Fresh Fabric Treats

---------- with your favorite Moda Bake Shop designers ----------

16 YUMMY PROJECTS TO SEW
FROM JELLY ROLLS, LAYER CAKES & MORE

stash BOOKS

an imprint of C&T Publishing

© 2011 by C&T Publishing, Inc.

...nge

...usanne Woods

...a Bix

...ical Editors: Ann Haley and Carolyn Aune

Book Designer: Kristen Yenche

Cover Designer/Design Director: Kristy Zacharias

Production Coordinator: Zinnia Heinzmann

Production Editor: Alice Mace Nakanishi

Illustrator: Mary Flynn

Photography by Christina Carty-Francis and Diane Pedersen of C&T Publishing, Inc., unless otherwise noted. How-to photos by individual contributors unless otherwise noted.

Published by Stash Books, an imprint of C&T Publishing, Inc., P.O. Box 1456, Lafayette, CA 94549

Library of Congress Cataloging-in-Publication Data

Fresh fabric treats : 16 yummy projects from jelly rolls, layer cakes & more--with your favorite Moda Bake Shop designers.

    p. cm.

ISBN 978-1-60705-351-4 (softcover)

1. Machine quilting--Patterns. 2. Patchwork--Patterns. 3. Quilting--Computer network resources. I. C&T Publishing. II. Title.

TT835.F748 2011

746.46'041--dc22

2010039159

Printed in China

10 9 8 7 6 5 4 3

F

FRESH

Contents

Introduction

I first became involved in the world of quiltmaking in the 1970s, when this traditional art form was experiencing an exciting renaissance—partly in response to the 1976 United States bicentennial celebrations. Today we're in the midst of another modern revival of this art form that is equally exciting.

In the 1970s, factors that contributed to the evolution of quiltmaking included the introduction of fine quilting by machine, and later, the longarm quilting machine. Both made quilting less time-consuming and more achievable.

An important factor in today's quiltmaking rebirth is the introduction of precut fabrics. Many people are turning to quilting as an outlet for creativity as well as a form of "therapy" in response to hectic, demanding modern lifestyles. Moda's precuts take some of the stress out of the process. By eliminating the need for lots of tedious and time-consuming rotary cutting, precuts enable a quiltmaker to complete piecing a project in a matter of days rather than weeks.

You'll see a selection of Moda precuts in this book (page 7). These precut fabrics come in different sizes for different applications. For example, Jelly Rolls are perfect for strip quilting, while Charm Squares and Layer Cakes are great for patchwork. And precuts are handy for making non-quilt projects, such as tote bags and pillows.

Mixing and matching the variety of precuts with Moda's beautiful and varied fabric collections creates endless possibilities. Whether you are making a traditional family heirloom, a museum-quality art quilt, or anything in between, precut fabrics can be all or part of your creation. Precuts are also excellent for beginning sewing and for quick and easy patterns.

If you are familiar with Moda Bake Shop (www.modabakeshop.com), you know that there we offer online patterns using precuts for so many creative projects, created by a group of talented designers. In this book, you will see exciting new patterns created by some of your favorite Bake Shop designers. There's something for everyone—from full-size quilts to sewing kits to a bag for carrying a laptop computer—and something for every skill level.

This book celebrates Moda precuts and all the great projects you can create with them. I hope our Moda precut fabrics make your sewing enjoyable and rewarding.

—Mark Dunn, owner and president of Moda Fabrics

EQUIVALENT MEASURES

It's time to cook up a special delight, and there's no easier way to do it than using precut fabrics. Toss in a few of these handy ingredients for instant sewing satisfaction.

1. **Fat Quarter Bundle:** Contains 1 of each print in a collection; each fat quarter is 18″ × 22″.

2. **Charm Pack:** Contains 42 squares; each Charm Square is 5″ × 5″.

3. **Dessert Roll:** Contains 10 strips, each 5″ × 45″.

4. **Honey Bun:** Contains 40 strips, each 1½″ × 45″.

5. **Jelly Roll:** Contains 40 strips, each 2½″ × 45″.

6. **Layer Cake:** Contains 42 squares, each 10″ × 10″.

7. **Turnover:** Contains 80 triangles 6″ (2 of each print in a collection).

April in Paris Quilt

CHEF: Lissa Alexander

YIELD: 1 quilt, finished size
57½″ × 57½″

What's not to love about Paris in the springtime? The city is awash with color—cherry and apple blossoms, daffodils, and other flowers in every variety. The colorful greens and floral prints in this quilt remind me of the colors of the Tuileries Gardens.

Ingredients

Foundation: 1 Layer Cake in Bella Solids

Strips: 1 Jelly Roll and 1 Honey Bun *or* scraps totaling 4 yards (If using scraps, cut them into assorted strips varying in width from 1″–2½″.)

Backing and binding: 3¾ yards fabric

- Cut 1 section 62″ × width of fabric for the backing.

- Cut 1 section 62″ × 22″ for the backing.

- Cut 4 lengthwise strips 2½″ × 62″ for the double-fold binding.

Batting: 62″ × 62″

Tip

Do you have a lot of scraps? Using 2 Layer Cakes as the foundation blocks will yield a quilt 8 blocks × 10 rows measuring 76½″ × 95½″.

Instructions

Note: All seam allowances are ¼″.

BLOCK ASSEMBLY

1. On one corner of the Layer Cake square, mark 1″ from each edge. Repeat on the opposite corner. These marks will be your placement guide for the first strip.

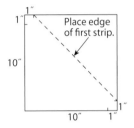

2. Start with a 14″-long strip. All other strips are various lengths. Align the first strip right side down diagonally along the 1″ marks. Each end of the strip should extend at least ½″ beyond the edge of the Layer Cake square.

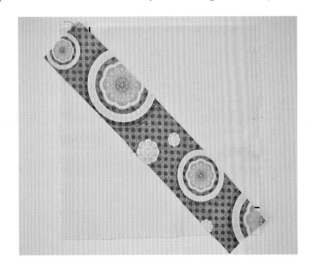

3. Sew ¼″ from the right edge of the strip. Turn the strip right side up and press. Add a 12″-long strip to the first strip, right sides together, leaving the solid-color foundation showing across the diagonal from corner to corner. Sew, flip, and press.

4. Repeat this process by adding additional strips. Continue sewing strips to the Layer Cake foundation square to the corner. The width of the strips can be determined as additional strips are added. If a strip is too wide for the area, lay the next strip in away from the raw edge of the previous strip and sew as shown below.

5. Repeat this process to cover the other half of the Layer Cake square. Begin with a strip that connects the two remaining 1″ marks. This will allow the foundation to show across the middle diagonal. Press the entire block.

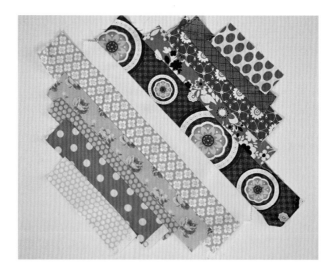

6. Place the block right side down. Square it up using the Layer Cake as your cutting guide. The block should measure 10″ × 10″ when trimmed. Make 36 blocks.

QUILT ASSEMBLY

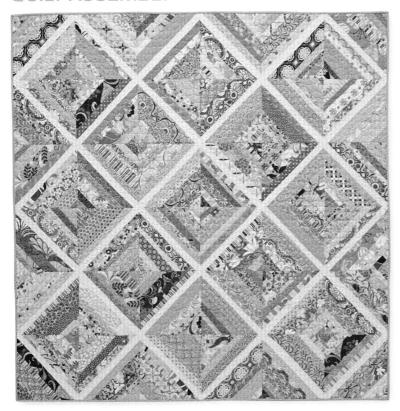

Sew 6 blocks together, alternating the direction of the solid diagonal strip, to form the first row. Press the seams open to avoid bulk at the corners. Repeat this process to make 6 rows. Join the rows together as shown in the project photo above.

FINISHING

Layer, baste, quilt, and bind using your favorite methods. For general finishing information, see Finishing Touches (page 121).

> **Tip**
> A string quilt pieced on a foundation fabric is a good candidate for tying instead of quilting. Tying is easy, quick, and a great opportunity to add small touches of color and interest with yarn or perle cotton.

Recipe:
Super Stars Quilt

CHEF: Amanda Jean Nyberg

YIELD: 1 quilt,
 finished size 72½″ × 72½″

Bold stars on a white background give you a golden opportunity to play with combining prints and solids.

Ingredients

1 Turnover for the star points

1 Charm Pack (with at least 36 charms 5″ × 5″) for the star centers

4 yards solid white / off-white for background, sashing, and borders

- Cut 6 strips 6″ × width of fabric; subcut into 36 squares 6″ × 6″. Cut in half on the diagonal to make 72 half-square triangles for the star points.

- Cut 5 strips 5″ × width of fabric. Subcut into 36 squares 5″ × 5″ for the corners of the Star blocks.

- Cut 1 piece 72½″ × fabric width; subcut as follows:

     Cut 2 pieces lengthwise 5″ × 72½″ for the final borders.

     Cut 4 pieces lengthwise 5″ × 63½″ for the sashing and borders.

     Cut 6 pieces 5″ × 18½″ for the sashing.

Binding: ¾ yard fabric

- Cut 8 strips 2½″ × 40″.

Backing: 4½ yards fabric

- Cut into 2 pieces 81″ long.

Batting: 80″ × 80″

Instructions

Note: All seam allowances are ¼″ unless noted.

BLOCK ASSEMBLY

1. Sew 72 Turnover pieces to 72 background half-square triangles. Press the seams open. Trim all half-square triangles to 5″ × 5″. Lay out each Star block as shown.

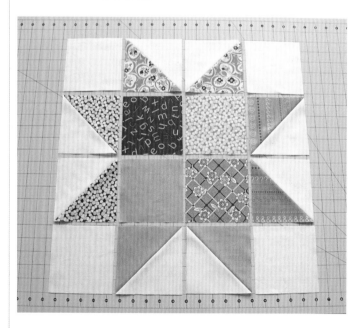

2. Sew the top 4 squares together and press the seams to the right. Sew the second row of squares together and press the seams to the left. Sew the third row of squares together and press the seams to the right. Sew the fourth row of squares together and press the seams to the left.

3. Assemble the rows together, pressing the seams toward the top of the block. Trim the block to 18½″ × 18½″.

4. Repeat Steps 1–3 to make a total of 9 Star blocks.

QUILT ASSEMBLY

1. Arrange the Star blocks in a 3-by-3 layout.

2. Place 5″ × 18½″ sashing strips vertically between the stars in each row.

3. Sew the pieces together to form the first row. Press the seams toward the sashing. Assemble the remaining 2 rows of stars in the same manner.

4. Add 5″ × 63½″ sashing pieces between the rows of stars and to the top and bottom. Press all seams toward the sashing.

5. Add the final 2 borders 5″ × 72½″ to the sides. Press the seams toward the sashing.

FINISHING

Layer, baste, quilt, and bind using your favorite methods. For general finishing information, see Finishing Touches (page 121).

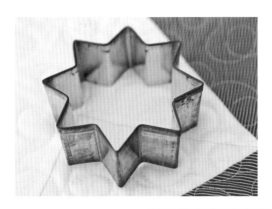

Flag Baby Quilt and Banner

CHEF: Vanessa Christenson

YIELD: 1 quilt, finished size 49″ × 49″;
1 banner, approximately 20′ long

Made in pastel fabrics, this quilt and banner are sweet baby's room projects. The colorful quilt flags and green bias strips are hand appliquéd to a simple muslin background; the banner sports the same flags.

Ingredients

This fabric amounts listed below are enough to make 1 quilt and 1 banner. I used fabrics from the Dream On collection by Urban Chiks.

Flags and inner border: 1 Layer Cake

Quilt top and borders: 1¾ yards white muslin (45″ wide)

- Cut 1 square 43″ × 43″ for the quilt top.

- Cut 5 strips 2½″ × 45″ for the outer borders.

Bias strips: 1¾ yards green stripe fabric

- Cut a 45″ × 45″ square. Then cut bias strips starting with the diagonal through the center of the square as follows:

    Cut 6 bias strips 1½″ wide for the quilt.

    Cut 6 bias strips 2½″ wide for the banner.

Backing: 3 yards coordinating fabric

Binding: ½ yard blue flowered fabric

- Cut 5 strips 2⅛″ wide for the binding.

Instructions

BABY QUILT
Appliqué

1. Fold each Layer Cake fabric square in half, right sides together, with the folded edge closest to you. Fold all 40 squares in the package.

2. Place a bowl or plate halfway on the folded layer block to make a semicircle approximately 8″ in diameter. Make sure you place it as far left as you can, leaving just enough for a seam allowance on the left edge (approximately ¼″). With a pencil or water-soluble marking pen, trace around your bowl or plate. Repeat this step for all 40 folded squares.

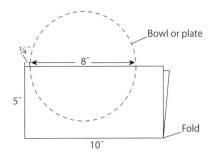

3. Sew on the traced line for each block. Cut out flags ¼″ outside the seam. Turn the flags inside out and press. Save the remnant of the square. You will use this later on for the inner borders of the quilt.

4. Set the flags on top of the 43″ × 43″ muslin square. Play around with the placement of the flags until you find a pleasing arrangement. I used 22 flags for my quilt. Pin the flags in place.

5. Place a pinned flag section in a big embroidery hoop. Appliqué flags onto the muslin. You can appliqué the whole flag or just the round part and do a running stitch on the straight side of the flag to keep it in place. The raw edges will be covered later by the green bias strips. Repeat for all the flags.

6. Join 6 green 1½″ × 40″ bias strips together with a diagonal seam. Fold the bias strip in half lengthwise with wrong sides together. Stitch along the long raw edges with a ⅛″ seam allowance. Press with the seam in the middle of the strip.

7. Pin the bias strip with the seam facing down onto the quilt top.

8. Using a large embroidery hoop, appliqué each edge of the bias strip to the quilt top. After you appliqué the first bias strip from one side of the quilt to the other side, trim the ends. Pin the next bias strip and repeat this step. Do this for each bias strip.

Borders

This quilt has a narrow inner border made with the Layer Cake remnants left after cutting the flag appliqués and a muslin outer border.

1. Cut the remnants from the flag squares into 1½″-wide strips.

2. To achieve a scrappy look, trim the 1½″-wide strips to different lengths. Sew the strips end to end to measure 1½″ × 43″. Make 2 strips. Sew the 1½″ × 43″ pieced strips to the left and right sides of the quilt top. Make 2 strips 1½″ × 45″ and attach them to the top and bottom of the quilt top.

3. Sew 2 white 2½″ × 45″ outer border strips to the left and right of the quilt top. Piece the remaining 2½″-wide strips to create 2 strips 2½″ × 49″. Sew the 2½″ × 49″ muslin strips to the top and bottom of the quilt top.

Finishing

Layer, baste, quilt, and bind using your favorite methods. For general finishing information, see Finishing Touches (page 121).

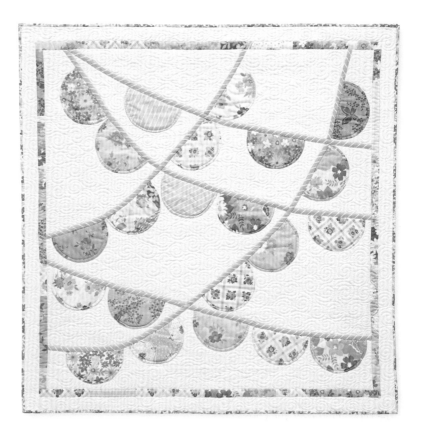

BANNER

With the approximately 20 remaining flags, you can make a pretty good size banner to hang in the room.

1. Sew 6 green 2½″-wide bias strips end to end to make one continuous strip. Press both long edges of the strip toward the middle. Fold again and press with an iron to finish your bias strip.

2. Place flags between the folds of the bias strip, starting no less than 12″ from the end. Pin in place. Sew your bias strip closed from end to end, encasing the open edge of the flags. Fold over the ends and sew them down to have finished ends on the bias strip.

Display the banner proudly, but for safety make certain to keep it out of reach of curious hands!

Recipe:
Rock Garden Quilt

CHEF: John Q. Adams

YIELD: 1 quilt,
finished size $59\frac{1}{2}'' \times 83\frac{1}{2}''$

This quilt is a modern take on the traditional Rail Fence quilt pattern. Made using a single Jelly Roll and coordinated solid fabrics, this pattern is updated by replacing several of the rails with the solid background color. Not only does this give the pattern more movement, it also effectively uses negative space to appeal to the more modern aesthetic. The project comes together quickly using chain-piecing techniques.

Ingredients

Blocks: 1 Jelly Roll (I used the Origins line by Basic Grey for Moda Fabrics.)

Background and inner border: 2 yards yellow fabric

- Cut 5 strips 2½″ × width of fabric for blocks.

- Cut 11 strips 4½″ × width of fabric for blocks and inner border.

- Cut 1 strip 2½″ × 12½″ for the final cobblestone block.

- Cut 1 strip 4½″ × 12½″ for the final cobblestone block.

Outer border: ½ yard green fabric

- Cut 7 strips 2″ × width of fabric.

Binding: ⅝ yard coordinating fabric

- Cut 7 strips 2½″ × width of fabric.

Backing: 4 yards coordinating fabric

- Cut 2 pieces 72″ × fabric width.

Batting: 72″ × 89″

Instructions

Note: All seam allowances are ¼″.

BLOCK ASSEMBLY

1. Select 33 Jelly Roll strips and separate them into 11 sets of 3 strips. Select your strip sets based on their level of contrast and overall aesthetic appeal.

2. Sew each set of strips together along the long (45″) edges. Press. Each strip set should measure 6½″ × 45″.

Tip

Though I typically press seams to one side in my quilting projects, I find that pressing seams open when sewing together long fabric strips helps to reduce distortion in the straight lines of the sets, which also makes squaring up my blocks later much easier.

Cobblestone (Vertical) Blocks

1. Select 5 of your strip sets to become your "cobblestone" blocks.

2. Sew a 4½″-wide strip of your background fabric to one side of each of the 5 strip sets.

3. Sew a 2½″-wide strip of your background fabric to the opposite side of each of these 5 strip sets. Each strip set should now measure 12½″ × 45″.

4. From each strip set, trim off the selvage edge and cut 3 blocks 12½″ × 12½″, for a total of 15 cobblestone blocks. Set aside. The sixteenth vertical cobblestone block will be made in Step 5 of the Stepping Stone (Horizontal) Blocks.

Stepping Stone (Horizontal) Blocks

1. Select 5 of your strip sets to become your horizontal "stepping stones" blocks.

2. From each strip set, trim off the selvage edge and cut 3 blocks 6½″ × 12½″ for a total of 15 cobblestone blocks.

3. From your final strip set, cut 2 blocks 6½″ × 12½″. One of these will be your sixteenth horizontal stepping stone block. Place it with the other stepping stone blocks.

4. Take the remaining 6½″ × 12½″ strip from Step 3 and add a 4½″ × 12½″ strip of the solid fabric to one side of it and a 2½″ × 12½″ strip to the other. This will be your sixteenth vertical cobblestone block.

QUILT ASSEMBLY

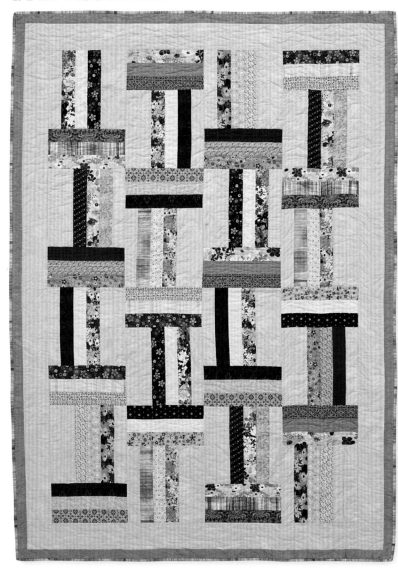

Lay out the blocks in vertical columns to assemble the quilt as follows.

1. In Column 1 (the far left column), start with a vertical cobblestone block and alternate the cobblestone blocks with horizontal stepping stone blocks. Your column should consist of 4 cobblestone blocks and 4 stepping stone blocks. When laying out the blocks, be sure to alternate the wider (4½″) strip of the background color on the cobblestone blocks from side to side with each block. Refer to the project photo (left) and assemble all the blocks in Column 1.

2. Lay out Column 2. This time, start with a stepping stone block and alternate stepping stone and cobblestone blocks. Sew together all the blocks in Column 2.

3. Construct columns 3 and 4 in the same manner. Column 3 starts with a cobblestone block, and Column 4 starts with a stepping stone block.

4. Once all 4 columns are assembled, sew them together to create the center of the quilt top, which will measure 48½″ × 72½″.

Inner Border

1. Trim the selvage edges off the 6 remaining 4½″-wide strips of your background fabric. Sew the strips together end to end.

2. From your continuous piece, cut 2 strips measuring 72½″ in length. Attach these strips to the 2 long sides of your quilt.

3. From your remaining piece, cut 2 more strips measuring 56½″ in length. Attach these strips to the top and bottom of your quilt.

Outer Border

1. Trim the selvage edges off the seven 2″-wide strips of your green outer border fabric. Sew your strips together end to end using a diagonal seam.

2. From your continuous piece, cut 2 strips measuring 80½″ in length. Attach these strips to the two long sides of your quilt.

3. From your remaining piece, cut 2 more strips measuring 59½″ in length. Attach these strips to the top and bottom of your quilt.

QUILTING AND FINISHING

Layer, baste, quilt, and bind using your favorite methods. For general finishing information, see Finishing Touches (page 121).

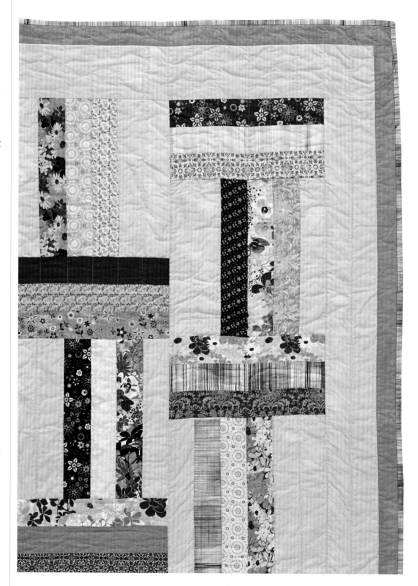

It's a Picnic Kind of Day Quilt

CHEF: Natalia Bonner

YIELD: 1 quilt,
finished size 63″ × 63″

On your next summer outing, spread out this cheery-looking quilt for your picnic.

Ingredients

I used Bella Solids (by Moda) plus additional Moda prints.

2 cream solid Charm Packs

- Cut 46 Charm Squares in half to get 92 rectangles, each 2½″ × 5″.

1 red solid Charm Pack

- Cut 1 Charm Square in half diagonally twice to create 4 small A triangles.
- Cut 6 Charm Squares in half diagonally once to create 12 C triangles.

1 red solid Jelly Roll

- Cut 2 red Jelly Roll strips into 32 squares 2½″ × 2½″. Take 8 of those squares and cut them in half diagonally once to create 16 B triangles.
- Trim 5 red Jelly Roll strips to 1½″ wide for the middle border. Trim 2 strips to 1½″ × 44″. Piece the remaining 3 strips to create 2 strips 1½″ × 46″.
- Cut 6 red Jelly Roll strips into 24 strips 2½″ × 9″ for the outer border sashing.
- Cut 2 red Jelly Roll strips into 8 strips 1½″ × 9″ for the outer border corner sashing.
- Cut 2 red Jelly Roll strips into 4 strips 2″ × 12″ for the outer border corners.

1 yard cream fabric (I used Bella Solids Natural.)

- Cut 4 strips 3¾″ × width of fabric for the inner border. Subcut to 2 strips 3¾″ × 37½″ and 2 strips 3¾″ × 44″.
- Cut 4 squares 9″ × 9″ for the outer border corners.

1 yard dark print fabric for the flower centers and binding (I used Essential Dots Black.)

- Cut 7 strips 2⅛″ × width of fabric for the binding.

4¾ yards yellow print fabric for the backing and flower appliqués (I used Dottie Butter.)

Batting: 71″ × 71″

Instructions

All seam allowances are ¼".

QUILT CENTER ASSEMBLY

1. Sew a red B triangle to either end of a 2½" × 5" cream rectangle as shown below to create Row 1. Make 2.

Row 1

2. Sew a 2½" × 5" cream rectangle to either side of a red Charm Square. Attach a C triangle to either side of this unit as shown below to create Row 2. Make 2.

Row 2

3. Sew 3 cream rectangles 2½" × 5" and 2 red squares 2½" × 2½" together, alternating colors. Attach a B triangle to either end of the strip to create Row 3. Make 2.

Row 3

4. Sew 4 cream rectangles 2½" × 5" and 3 red Charm Squares together, alternating colors. Attach a red C triangle to either end to create Row 4. Make 2.

Row 4

5. Create Row 5 using 5 cream rectangles 2½" × 5", 4 red squares 2½" × 2½", and 2 B triangles. Make 2.

Row 5

6. Create Row 6 using 6 cream rectangles 2½" × 5", 5 red Charm Squares, and 2 C triangles. Make 2.

Row 6

7. Create Row 7 using 7 cream rectangles 2½" × 5", 6 red squares 2½" × 2½", and 2 B triangles. Make 2.

Row 7

8. Make the center row (Row 8) using 8 cream rectangles 2½" × 5", 7 red Charm Squares, and 2 A triangles. Make 1.

Row 8—Make 1.

9. Assemble the center panel by joining the rows as shown. Pay close attention to the orientation of the triangles at either end of each row. Add an A triangle to each Row 1 to complete the quilt center, which should measure approximately 37¼" × 37¼" before the borders are added.

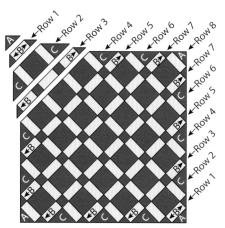
Center Assembly Diagram

BORDERS

Inner Borders

1. Add a 3⅞″ × 37¼″ cream strip to either side of the quilt center. Sew a 3⅞″ × 44″ cream strip to the top and bottom.

2. Add a 1½″ × 44″ red strip to each side of the quilt top. Sew a 1½″ × 46″ red strip to the top and bottom.

Outer Border

1. Sew a 2½″ × 5″ red rectangle to the top of a cream Charm Square. Sew a 2½″ × 5″ cream rectangle to the top of the red rectangle to create a border unit. Make 28.

2. Create 1 outer border by alternating 7 border units with 6 red strips 2½″ × 9″. Add a red 1½″ × 9″ strip to both ends. Make 4.

3. Measure 3¾″ from the corner of a 9″ × 9″ square of cream fabric and make a cut as shown below. Measure another 1″ and make another cut. Repeat with the remaining 3 squares 9″ × 9″.

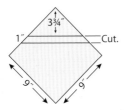

4. Discard the 1″ strip from Step 3 and insert a 2″ × 12″ red strip. Trim the ends even with the square. Repeat to make 4 squares.

5. Measure 1¾″ from the bottom of the red strip and make another cut. Repeat with the remaining squares.

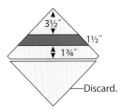

6. Add 1 outer border from Step 2 to the left and right side of the quilt top.

7. Sew a corner unit from Step 5 to each end of the remaining 2 outer borders. Attach to the top and bottom of the quilt.

8. Cut 8 A flowers, 8 B flowers and 8 C flowers and their respective flower centers using the template patterns on pages 35–36.

9. Using the appliqué method of your choice, add 6 flowers to each side of your border. I used a starch appliqué method and a machine blanket stitch with black thread to appliqué my flowers.

10. Enlarge the templates 200% for "It's a picnic kind of day" (pages 37–38). Use the appliqué method of your choice to appliqué the words to one inner border, as shown in the project photo (page 34).

FINISHING

Layer, baste, quilt, and bind using your favorite methods. For general finishing information, see Finishing Touches (page 121).

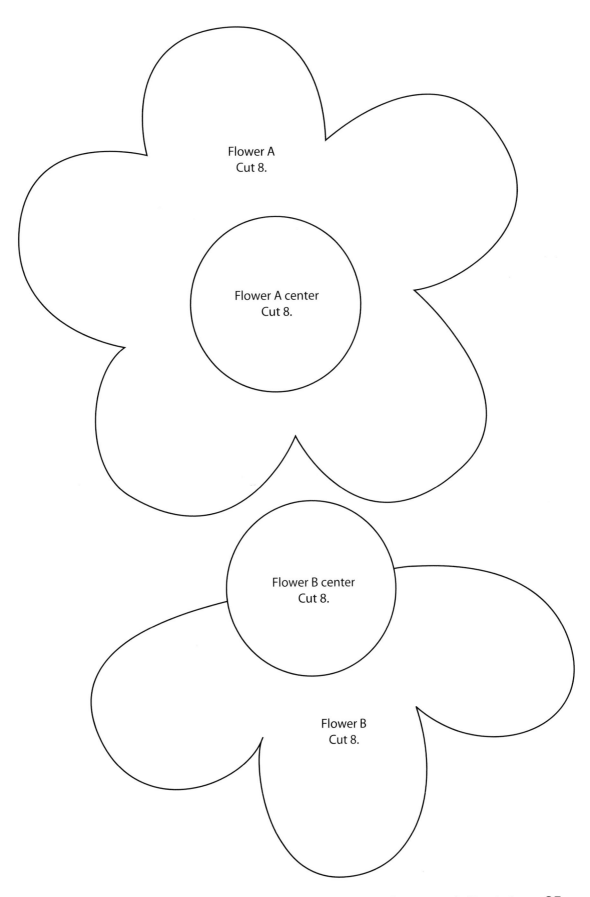

Flower A
Cut 8.

Flower A center
Cut 8.

Flower B center
Cut 8.

Flower B
Cut 8.

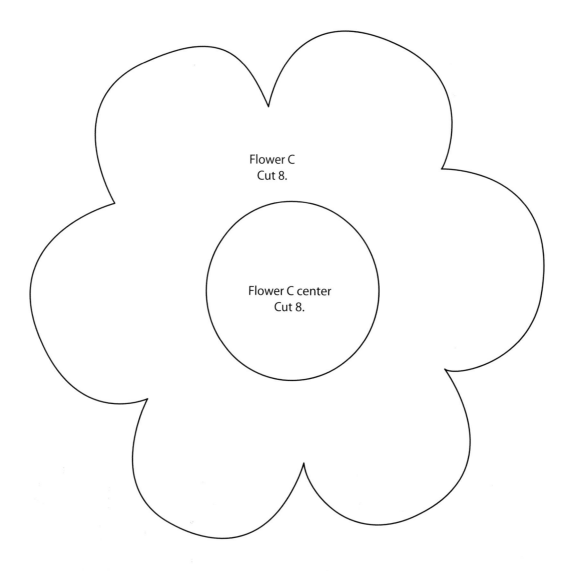

Flower C
Cut 8.

Flower C center
Cut 8.

it's
a
picnic

Enlarge 200%.

kind
of
day.

Enlarge 200%.

Recipe:
Wonky Nine-Patch Quilt

CHEF: Vickie Eapen

YIELD: 1 quilt, finished size
48½″ × 48½″
(finished block size 8″ × 8″)

The sum of nine-patches and single solid blocks adds up to a colorful quilt that's quick and easy to make.

Ingredients

Wonky Nine Patch blocks: 1 Layer Cake of print fabrics (I used Happy by Me and My Sister.)

Outer blocks: 1 Layer Cake of solid fabrics

- Cut 4 solid purple squares 8½″ × 8½″.

- Cut 4 solid pink squares 8½″ × 8½″.

- Cut 4 solid yellow squares 8½″ × 8½″.

- Cut 4 solid green squares 8½″ × 8½″.

Sashing and binding: 1 Jelly Roll white solid

- Cut 4 white Jelly Roll strips into 20 strips 2½″ × 8½″ for the vertical sashing.

- Piece 5 white Jelly Roll strips together end to end and cut into 4 strips 2½″ × 48½″ for horizontal sashing.

- Use 5 white Jelly Roll strips (2½″ × 45″) for the double-fold binding.

Backing: 3¼ yards fabric

Batting: 56″ × 56″

Instructions

Note: All seam allowances are ¼″.

BLOCK ASSEMBLY

1. Stack 9 of the print Layer Cake fabrics neatly. Make 2 cuts through all layers to create ⅓ segments as shown.

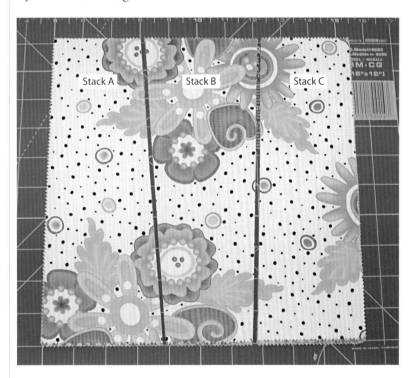

2. The fabric stack on the left is stack A. Move the top fabric of stack B to the bottom of the stack. Move the top 2 fabrics of stack C to the bottom of the stack.

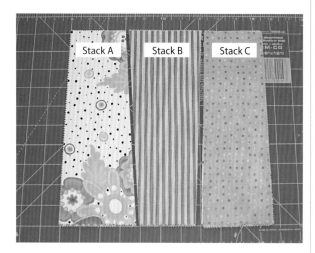

3. Sew A to B for all 9 sets. Sew AB's to C's for all 9 sets. It is very important to keep these in order while sewing.

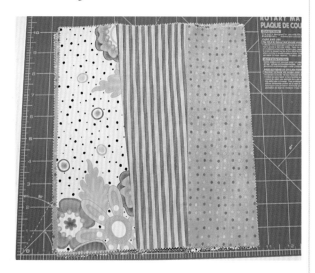

4. Stack your squares neatly one on top of the other. Turn 90° and cut again into ⅓ segments.

5. Label the stacks left to right as D, E, and F. From the stack E, take the first 3 fabrics and move them to the bottom of the stack. From the stack F, take the first 6 fabrics and move them to the bottom of the stack.

6. Sew D to E for all 9 blocks. Sew DE's to F's for all 9 blocks.

7. Trim all 9 blocks to 8½″ × 8½″.

QUILT ASSEMBLY

1. Using the project photo for reference, arrange the pieced 8½″ × 8½″ blocks in a nine-patch grid with the solid 8½″ × 8½″ blocks around the perimeter.

2. Join each of the blocks in the top row, adding a 2½″ × 8½″ white sashing strip between blocks (see Assembly Diagram, below). Repeat to create 5 rows.

3. Join the 5 rows with a 2½″ × 48½″ white sashing strip between each row as shown in the Assembly Diagram.

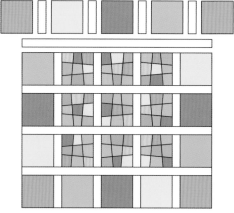

Assembly Diagram

FINISHING

Layer, baste, quilt, and bind using your favorite methods. For general finishing information, see Finishing Touches (page 121).

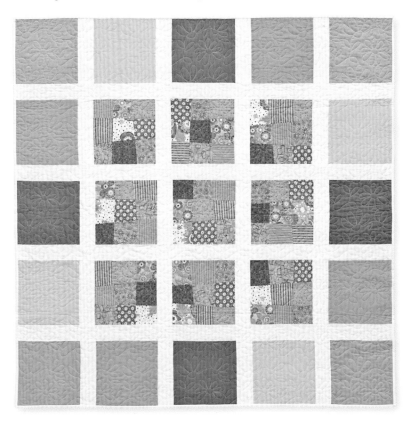

Summer Sorbet Quilt

CHEF: Rachel Griffith
Quilted by: Darla Padilla

YIELD: 1 quilt, finished size 80″ × 80″
(finished block size 13½″ × 13½″)

Bright stars twinkle among colorful nine-patch squares in this fun summery quilt that combines prints and solids in an easy-to-make design.

Ingredients

2 print Charm Packs (I used Fandango.)

3 neutral solids Charm Packs (I used Bella Oatmeal.)

3 pastel solids Charm Packs (I used Bella Warm Pastels.)

½ yard aqua fabric for the inner border

- Cut 8 strips 1½″ × 45″.

1½ yards coral fabric for the outer border

- Cut 8 strips 5½″ × 45″.

¾ yard fabric for the binding

- Cut 8 strips 2½″ × width of fabric.

5 yards fabric for the backing

Batting: 88″ × 88″

Instructions

All seam allowances are ¼″.

BLOCK ASSEMBLY

This quilt features 12 Star blocks and 13 Nine Patch blocks.

Star Blocks

1. Select 12 print Charm Squares for the Star block centers; set aside.

2. Cut 48 print Charm Squares in half diagonally to make 96 triangles.

3. Layer a print triangle on top of a solid neutral Charm Square with right sides together. Place it so it's slightly askew. Stitch along the long side of the triangle, using a ¼″ seam allowance. Cut off the excess solid neutral Charm Square.

4. Press the print fabric open.

5. Trim unit to a 5″ × 5″ square.

6. Layer a contrasting print triangle on top of your pieced Charm Square. Stitch along the long side of the triangle. Trim off the excess background Charm Square.

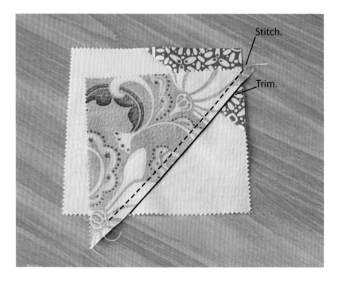

Stitch.

Trim.

7. Press the print fabric open. Trim it back down to a 5″ × 5″ square to finish the star point unit. Make 48 star point units total.

Finished star point square

8. Arrange 1 reserved print Charm Square, 4 star point units, and 4 assorted neutral solid Charm Squares, as shown. Sew together as a Nine Patch block. Each completed Star block should measure 14″ × 14″. Make 12 Star blocks.

Nine Patch Blocks

Sew 9 solid pastel Charm Squares to form a basic Nine Patch block. Each completed Nine Patch block should measure 14″ × 14″. Make 13 Nine Patch blocks.

QUILT ASSEMBLY

1. Arrange all the blocks on a design wall, alternating Star blocks and Nine Patch blocks, as shown in the photo (left). Sew into rows and then sew all the rows together to create the quilt top center. The quilt top center should measure 68″ × 68″.

2. Sew 4 aqua 1½″ × 45″ inner border strips together end to end to create 1 long strip. Make 2. Cut a 1½″ × 68″ strip from each strip and sew to the sides of the quilt top center. Cut a 1½″ × 70″ strip from each remaining long strip and sew to the top and bottom of the quilt top.

3. Sew 4 coral 5½″ × 45″ outer border strips together end to end to create 1 long strip. Make 2. Cut a 5½″ × 70″ strip from each long strip and sew to the sides of the quilt top. Cut a 5½″ × 80″ strip from the remaining long strips and sew to the top and bottom of the quilt top.

QUILTING AND FINISHING

Layer, baste, quilt, and bind using your favorite methods. For general finishing information, see Finishing Touches (page 121).

Recipe:
Block Holder Books

CHEF: Julie Herman

YIELD: 2 block holder books, finished sizes
11$\frac{1}{4}$″ × 11$\frac{1}{2}$″ (small)
and 20$\frac{1}{4}$″ × 20$\frac{1}{2}$″ (large)

These block holder books have flannel "pages" that keep your projects neat and tidy. They work very well for block-of-the-month projects or blocks with lots of pieces. I often use them to go back and forth to classes and sewing nights.

Ingredients

In this project I used precuts of Punctuation by American Jane. The quantities listed below are sufficient to make 1 large and 1 small block holder book.

Read all project instructions before cutting so that you can choose where you want to place each color strip.

Bold Exterior blocks: 1 Charm Pack

Borders and ties: 1 Honey Bun

- Cut 4 strips 1½" × 9½" for small block border sides.

- Cut 4 strips 1½" × 11½" for small block border tops and bottoms.

- Cut 4 strips 1½" × 18½" for large block border sides.

- Cut 4 strips 1½" × 20½" for large lock border tops and bottoms.

- Select and set aside 5 Honey Bun strips for ties.

Backing: 1¼ yards green print fabric

- Cut 1 rectangle 26" × 15" for the small block holder book.

- Cut 1 rectangle 44" × 24" for the large block holder book.

Binding: ½ yard white stripe fabric

- Cut 6 strips 2½" × 40".

Batting: 40" × 44"

- Cut 1 rectangle 26" × 15" for the small block holder book.

- Cut 1 rectangle 44" × 24" for the large block holder book.

Pages: 2¼ yards off-white flannel (Cut all flannel with pinking shears or use a pinking blade for your rotary cutter.)

- Cut 3 rectangles 20" × 10" for the small block holder book.

- Cut 3 rectangles 38" × 19" for the large block holder book.

Pinking shears or a pinking blade for your rotary cutter

Safety pins

Instructions

Note: All seam allowances are ¼".

UNIT ASSEMBLY

1. Arrange 40 squares from the Charm Pack to make 2 Four-Patch blocks and 2 Sixteen-Patch blocks.

2. Sew the Four-Patch blocks. Make 2. Sew the Sixteen-Patch blocks. Make 2.

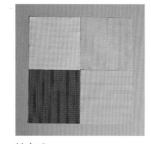

Make 2.   Make 2.

3. Audition 2 Honey Bun strips 1½″ × 9½″ and 2 strips 1½″ × 11½″ to border each small block. Repeat with 2 Honey Bun strips 1½″ × 18½″ and 2 strips 1½″ × 20½″ for the large blocks.

4. Sew the side strips to the small block and press the seams toward the border. Repeat for the top and bottom strips. Make 2 small blocks. Repeat to border the 2 large blocks.

5. Sew the small blocks together along one side. Repeat for the large blocks.

Completed small unit exterior

TIES

Fold a 1½″ × 45″ tie strip in half, right sides together so it measures 1½″ × 22½″. Sew a ¼″ seam along each side. Trim the seam allowances and selvages. Pin a safety pin at one end of the tie and work it back through the inside of the tie. Pull to turn the tie inside out and remove the safety pin. Press and tie a knot at each end to finish the raw edges. Repeat to make a total of 5 ties.

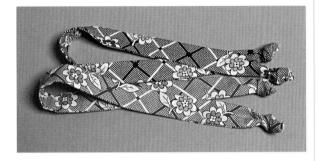

QUILTING

For information about layering, basting, quilting, and binding, refer to Finishing Touches (page 121).

1. Layer the 26″ × 15″ green print backing fabric, 26″ × 15″ batting, and small block holder book, and baste. Quilt by hand or machine. I did a basic stitch in-the-ditch around all the units using a walking foot. Repeat layering and quilting the large block holder book using the 44″ × 24″ backing fabric and the 44″ × 24″ batting.

2. Bind each block holder book.

FINISHING

1. Place the completed small unit with the backing facing up and layer the 3 small pieces of flannel on top. Pin the flannel to the small unit, avoiding the center.

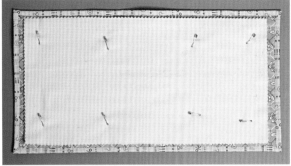

2. Turn the unit over. Center and pin 1 tie in place 2¼″ from the top edge. Center and pin another tie 2¼″ from the bottom edge. Using a walking foot, sew down the center of the unit. Backstitch at the start and end of this stitching. This stitching secures the flannel "pages" and the ties all at the same time.

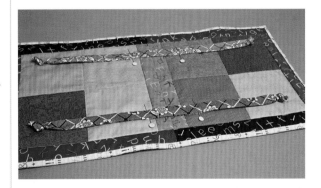

3. Repeat Steps 1 and 2 to complete the large block holder book, using the large pieces of flannel. In Step 2, place 1 tie 3″ from the top, another tie 3″ from the bottom, and the third one in the center.

Recipe:
Gathered Table Runner

CHEF: Sweetwater

YIELD: 1 table runner,
finished size 42½″ × 16″

Simple but sophisticated, this table runner features alternating rows of quilted and gathered strips in a mix of perfectly coordinated prints.

Ingredients

I used Pure Sweetwater fabrics by Moda.

Center: 19 Jelly Roll strips

- Cut 10 strips 2½″ × 12″.
- Cut 9 strips 2½″ × 24″.

Borders: ⅜ yard fabric

- Cut 2 strips 2½″ × 38½″.
- Cut 2 strips 2½″ × 16″.

Binding: ⅓ yard (or use leftover Jelly Roll strips)

- Cut 4 strips 2¼″ × 45″ each.

Backing: ⅔ yard fabric for the backing

- Cut 1 rectangle 20″ × 45″.

Batting: 20″ × 46″

Instructions

Note: ¼″ seam allowance is included.

BACKGROUND

1. Set the stitch length on the sewing machine to the longest length. Run a gathering stitch ⅛″ from each long side of the 2½″ × 24″ background strips. Pull up the gathers on one side to measure 12″.

2. With the right sides together, sew the gathered side to one of the 2½″ × 12″ strips.

3. Pull up the gathers on the other side of the 24″ strip to measure 12″. With the right sides together, sew the gathered strip to one of the 2½″ × 12″ flat strips.

4. Repeat the above steps until all of the gathered strips and the flat strips are sewn together. Alternate 10 flat strips with 9 gathered strips to create the center of the table runner.

BORDERS

1. Sew the 2½″ × 38½″ border strips to the top and bottom of the table runner.

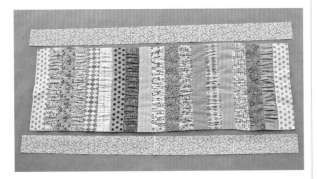

2. Sew the 2½″ × 16″ border strips to either end of the table runner.

FINISHING

Layer, baste, quilt, and bind using your favorite methods. For general finishing information, see Finishing Touches (page 121).

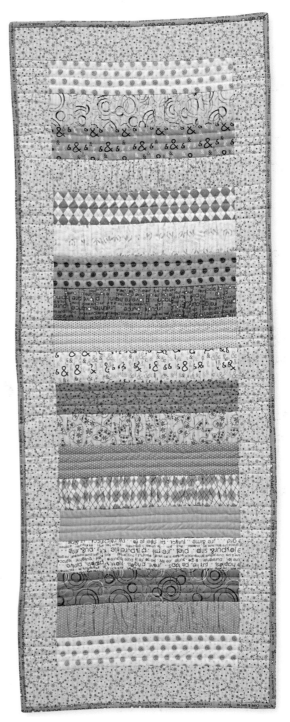

Recipe:
Vintage Postage Stamp Pillow

CHEF: Angela Yosten

YIELD: 1 pillow, finished size 18˝ × 18˝
(approximately 24˝ × 24˝ with ruffle)

I am inspired by everyday items when I design something new. As a child, I loved to collect vintage stamps and found all the different designs and markings fascinating. For this pillow design, I was inspired by a 1960 Abraham Lincoln airmail stamp; I added a touch of ruffled edge to resemble the wavy edge of a stamp. I hope you enjoy it!

Ingredients

Pillow front and back: 1 Jelly Roll (I used Maison De Garance by French General), divided into red and cream colorways

- Cut 7 cream Jelly Roll strips 2½″ × 15½″ for the front center.

- Cut 1 red Jelly Roll strip 2½″ × 15½″; subcut in half lengthwise to create 2 strips 1¼″ × 15½″ for the front center.

- Cut 2 red strips 2½″ × 15″ for the top and bottom borders.

- Cut 2 red strips 2½″ × 19″ for the side borders.

- Cut 9 cream Jelly Roll strips to 2½″ × 20″ for the back.

- Cut 2 red Jelly Roll strips to 2½″ × 20″ for the back.

Back lining: ½ yard coordinating solid fabric

- Cut 1 piece 12½″ × 20″ and 1 piece 10½″ × 20″.

Ruffle: 1 yard coordinating print fabric

- Cut 4 strips 7″ × fabric width.

Ties: 2 yards of ⅜″-wide coordinating grosgrain ribbon or twill tape

- Cut 6 pieces of grosgrain ribbon to 12″ each.

Fusible webbing: ½ yard (I recommend Wonder Under by Pellon.)

18″ × 18″ pillow form

Instructions

All seam allowances are ¼″ unless otherwise noted.

1. Lay out the pillow front strips, long edges together, from top to bottom as follows:

> 3 cream strips 2½″ × 15½″
>
> 1 red strip 1¼″ × 15½″
>
> 1 cream strip 2½″ × 15½″
>
> 1 red strip 1¼″ × 15½″
>
> 3 cream strips 2½″ × 15½″

2. Sew all the strips together. Press all the seams in one direction. Topstitch along the side of the seam with the seam allowance.

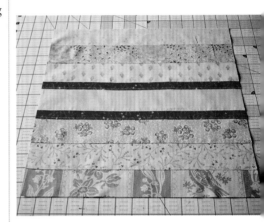

3. Trim assembled section to 15″ × 15″, taking an equal amount from the top and bottom.

4. Sew a red 2½″ × 15″ strip to the top and bottom of the pillow front.

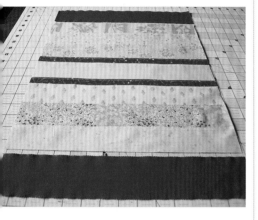

5. Sew a red 2½″ × 19″ strip to the left and right sides of the pillow front. Trim the pillow top to 19″ × 19″ square.

APPLIQUÉ

1. Select 4 red print Jelly Roll strips and sew them together along the 45″ edges to create an 8½″ × 45″ strip set. Press all the seams in one direction. Topstitch along each seam on the side with the seam allowance underneath. This will become your appliqué fabric.

2. Enlarge the patterns 200% (page 64) and use to create the templates. Reverse the templates and place on the paper side of the fusible web. Trace around each letter with a marker, pen, or fabric pencil.

Hint: I like to make sure my letters are angled and lying across 2 or more fabric prints to give the finished piece a scrappy or pieced look.

3. Following the manufacturer's directions, apply the fusible web to the wrong side of the appliqué strip set created in Step 1.

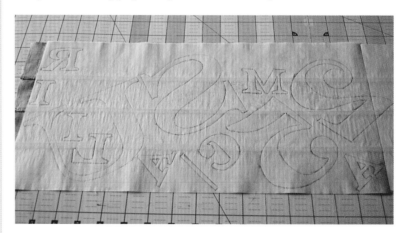

4. Carefully cut out the letters and peel off the paper backing. Position the letters on the pillow front and fuse them into place. Using a small blanket stitch, machine appliqué all the fused pieces into place.

PILLOW BACK

1. For the bottom half of the pillow back, sew 5 of the 2½″ × 20″ cream strips together, press the seams in one direction, and topstitch along the seams. Fold the piece in half twice to create 3 fold marks. Place a piece of ribbon at the top of each of the 3 fold marks, aligning with the raw edge of the fabric.

2. Place 1 of the red strips right sides together, aligning the top raw edges and sandwiching the ribbon between. Pin and stitch into place.

3. Fold the red strip up, press, and topstitch along the side of the seam with the seam allowance underneath.

4. Place the 12½″ × 20″ lining fabric and the bottom half of the pillow back right sides together.

5. Stitch along the top of the half pillow back and press the seam open.

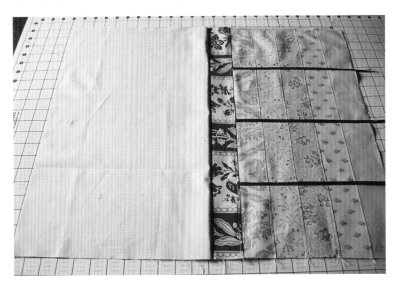

6. Fold the solid piece toward the back, matching wrong sides together. Press and topstitch along the folded top edge.

7. For the top half of the pillow back, sew 4 of the 2½″ × 20″ cream strips together; then add a red strip to the bottom edge. Press the seams in one direction and topstitch along the seams. Fold the piece in half twice, creating 3 fold marks.

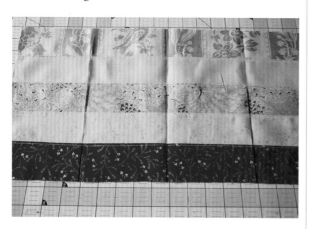

8. Place a piece of ribbon at the bottom of each of the 3 fold marks, aligning with the raw edge of the fabric. Place the 10½″ × 20″ lining fabric right sides together, aligning the bottom edge. Pin in place.

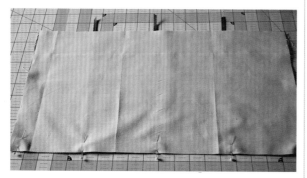

9. Stitch along the bottom edge of the pillow back and press the seams open. Fold the solid piece toward the back, matching wrong sides together. Press and topstitch the bottom folded edge in place.

10. Match up the 2 back halves as shown, overlapping the 2 red strips so that the ribbons match up evenly.

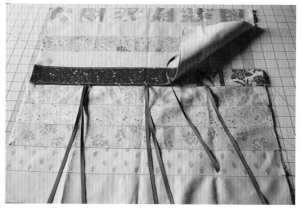

11. Tie bows in the 3 locations of the ribbon so your backing does not shift and so your ribbon does not get caught in the seams when you are sewing the front and back together.

12. Trim your pillow back to 19″ × 19″, taking an even amount from each side and making sure to keep it square. Set it aside.

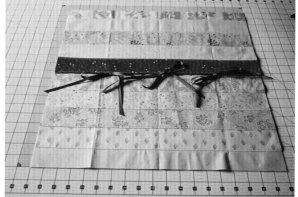

RUFFLE

1. Sew 4 ruffle strips 7″ × 45″ end to end, creating one large loop. Be sure not to twist the fabric when stitching the ends together. Fold and press the loop in half lengthwise with wrong sides together.

2. Sew a gathering stitch by setting your machine stitch width to the longest setting possible. Backstitch only at one end and sew along ⅛″ from the raw edges. From the end you did not backstitch, begin pulling the bottom thread to create a gather all the way around the loop.

3. Match the corners of the pillow front to the seams in the ruffle. Pin the ruffle to the right side of the pillow front. Adjust the ruffles so the gathers are evenly distributed and the ruffles lie flat.

4. Place the pillow back upside down with the right sides facing the pillow front, sandwiching the ruffle in between the front and back of the pillow. Pin in place. Using a ½″ seam allowance, sew around all 4 sides of the pillow. Make sure not to catch the ribbon in any of the seams. You do not need to leave an opening for turning since there is the opening in the back side of the pillow.

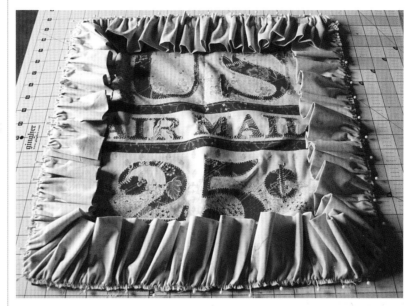

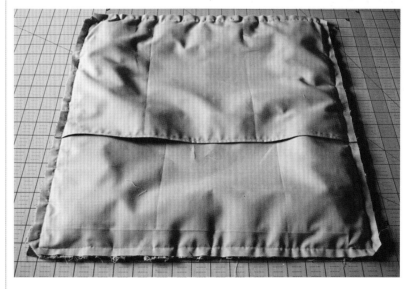

5. Reach through the back side opening and untie the ribbons. Flip the pillow right sides out. Stuff the pillow with an 18″ square pillow form, tie the ribbons off, and you're done!

US
AIR MAIL
25¢

Enlarge 200%.

Recipe:
Pack 'N' Go Tote

CHEF: Kimberly Walus

YIELD: 1 tote,
finished size 14″ × 10⅝″ × 6″

Pack up this roomy bag with your sewing supplies and go out the door to your next quilting adventure. If you wish, make the matching Make Life Sewing Kit (page 74) and pop it inside too.

Ingredients

I used precuts and yardage from Make Life by Sweetwater.

Exterior pockets: 1 Jelly Roll (A 10″ × 10″ Layer Cake will also work.)

- Select 20 strips and cut 1 rectangle 2½″ × 9″ from each Jelly Roll strip. Use leftover strips in other projects—or to make another tote.

Exterior: ⅔ yard multicolor print

- Cut 2 rectangles 6½″ × 11″ for the sides.

- Cut 2 rectangles 14½″ × 11″ for the front and back.

- Cut 1 rectangle 14½″ × 6½″ for the bottom.

Lining: 1 yard paisley print

- Cut 2 rectangles 6½″ × 9″ for the side pocket.

- Cut 2 rectangles 14½″ × 9″ for the front and back pockets.

- Cut 2 rectangles 6½″ × 11″ for the sides.

- Cut 2 rectangles 14½″ × 11″ for the front and back.

- Cut 1 rectangle 14½″ × 6½″ for the bottom.

Handles: ½ yard blue polka dot fabric

- Cut 2 strips 6″ × 40″.

Binding: ½ yard brown and blue striped fabric

- Cut 6 or 7 strips 2½″ wide on the bias. Piece together enough bias strips to create a strip at least 135″ long.

Batting: ⅝ yard 90″ wide (I used Warm and Natural cotton batting.)

- Cut 2 rectangles 6½″ × 9″ for the side pockets.

- Cut 2 rectangles 14½″ × 9″ for the front and back pockets.

- Cut 2 rectangles 6½″ × 11″ for the sides.

- Cut 2 rectangles 14½″ × 11″ for the front and back.

- Cut 1 rectangle 14½″ × 6½″ for the bottom.

- Cut 2 strips 1½″ × 40″ for the tote handles.

Garnishes

4 fabric-covered buttons (size 1⅛″)

Instructions

Seam allowances are ¼" unless otherwise noted.

FRONT, BACK, AND SIDE POCKETS

1. Arrange 20 strips 2½" × 9" in a pleasing manner from left to right. Divide the strips from left to right into 4 separate groups: 7 strips for the front pocket, 3 for the side pocket, 7 for the back pocket, and 3 for the other side pocket.

2. Place a piece of batting measuring 14½" × 9" on a table. Starting from the left, pick up 2 strips. Place the first strip on top of the batting with the right side of the fabric facing up. Place the second strip on top of the first strip with right sides together. Sew along the right edge with a ¼" seam. Open and press the seam to the right.

3. Place the third strip on top of the second strip with right sides together. Sew a ¼" seam along the right edge. Open and press the seam to the right. Repeat this process through strip 7. This completes the front pocket.

4. Place a piece of batting measuring 6½" × 9" on a table. Starting from the left, place the eighth strip on top of the batting with the right side of the fabric facing up. Place the ninth strip on top of the eighth strip with right sides together. Sew a ¼" seam along the right edge. Open and press the seam to the right.

5. Place the tenth strip on top of the ninth strip with right sides together. Sew a ¼" seam along the right edge. Open and press the seam to the right. This completes the side of the pocket.

6. Repeat this process for the back pocket and the other side pocket. From left to right number your pocket pieces 1–4.

7. Sandwich the Jelly Roll strip pocket, batting, and pocket lining, with the wrong side of the lining fabric facing the batting. Using your decorative sewing stitches, sew a different stitch pattern on the seamline between each strip. Using a straight stitch, sew down the middle of each strip. Trim the front and back pocket pieces to 14½" × 8". Trim the 2 side pocket pieces to 6½" × 8".

Add Binding to Pockets

1. From the 2½″ × 135″ bias strip, cut 2 pieces measuring 2½″ × 14½″ for the front and back pocket binding. Cut 2 bias strips measuring at least 2½″ × 6½″ for the side pocket binding. Fold each strip in half, with wrong sides together, and press.

2. Line up the raw edges of the binding along the top edge of the pocket. Sew on the binding using a ⅜″ seam allowance. Fold the binding up and over the top to the back. Press. Hand stitch or sew the binding in place by stitching in-the-ditch on the front of the pocket. Set aside.

HANDLES

1. Fold a 6″ × 40″ tote handle in half lengthwise with wrong sides together and press. Open and fold one raw edge toward the center and press. Place a piece of batting measuring 1½″ × 40″ inside the folded fabric you just pressed. Fold the other raw edge toward the center and press.

2. Fold the 2 sides together, encasing the raw edges and the batting inside. Topstitch the open edge closed using a ⅛″ seam allowance. Topstitch again using a ⅜″ seam allowance. Repeat topstitching for the opposite side of the tote handle.

3. Repeat Steps 1 and 2 for the other tote handle. Set aside.

EXTERIOR PANELS AND BOTTOM

1. Place the 14½″ × 11″ print fabric piece right side facing up on top of a 14½″ × 11″ batting rectangle.

2. Using a marking pencil and a ruler, mark a vertical line 1¼″ from the left edge (and parallel to the left edge). Mark another line 1″ to the right of the first line. Continue to mark quilting lines, 1″ apart, across the entire tote front.

3. Using a straight stitch, quilt along each line (refer to photo, bottom left, page 70).

4. Repeat Steps 1–3 for the back and side pieces.

5. Repeat Steps 1–3 for the bottom tote piece.

ATTACH HANDLES AND POCKETS

1. For the handle placement, measure 2¾″ from the left and right outside raw edges of the 14½″ × 11″ front quilted tote piece.

2. The long outside edge of the handle should line up along the 2¾″ measurements, and the raw end of the handle will line up with the bottom raw edge of the front quilted tote piece. Pin in place.

3. Measure up 8″ from the bottom raw edge of each side of the tote handles and mark it with a pin. Sew the handles in place by sewing along the handle, topstitching on one edge of the tote handle, then across at the 8″ pin mark, and then down the other side of the tote handle. Repeat for the opposite end of the handle.

4. Repeat Steps 1–3 for the back quilted tote piece.

5. Attach the pockets to the quilted tote panels. Place the lining side of the front pocket on the right side of the tote front. Baste the pockets along the sides and bottom using a ¼″ seam allowance. Repeat with the back and sides.

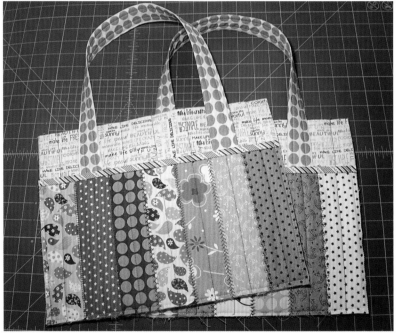

ASSEMBLE TOTE PANELS

1. Find the center of the bottom edge of each piece of the tote and mark with a pencil.

2. Lay out your 4 pieces from left to right in this order: front, side, back, side.

With right sides together, sew the front piece and side pieces using a ⅜″ seam, making sure to match up the tops of the pocket. Stop sewing ⅜″ from the bottom of each seam and backstitch. Press the seams open.

Sew the back to the remaining edge of the side. Press the seams open. Take the last side piece and sew it to the back piece. Press the seams open. Sew the last 2 pieces together, forming a circle. Press the seams open.

3. Take the 6½″ × 14½″ bottom that you previously quilted and find the center of each side and mark it with a pencil.

4. Turn the bag inside out and match up the pencil marks on the tote to the pencil marks on the quilted bottom fabric piece. Make a mark in each corner of the bottom piece by measuring ⅜″ from each corner. Sew using a ⅜″ seam allowance around the 4 sides of the bottom of the tote, making sure to stop at the corner marks and backstitch. Remove it from the machine and turn it to line up the next seam. Continue sewing in this manner until the remaining 3 sides are sewn. Turn right side out and set aside.

LINING

1. Find the center of the bottom edge of each lining piece (front, back, and sides) and mark it with a pencil.

2. Lay out the 4 lining pieces from left to right in this order: front, side, back, side. Using a ⅜″ seam allowance, sew the 4 pieces together in that order. Stop ⅜″ from the bottom of each seam. Press the seams open.

3. Find the center of each side of the lining bottom and mark it with a pencil. Turn the lining inside out and match up the centers marked in pencil; then match up the corners.

4. Sew around the 4 sides of the bottom of the lining. Keep the lining inside out.

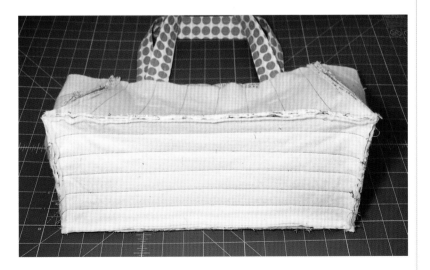

POCKET LOOP CLOSURES

1. Cut 4 pieces from the long bias strip to measure 2½″ × 10″ each.

2. Fold each piece in half lengthwise, with wrong sides together, and press. Open and fold the raw edges in toward the pressed fold and press. Close and press again.

3. Topstitch ⅛″ from each long edge of the folded bias strip.

4. Repeat Steps 2–3 for the other 3 pocket closures.

5. Fold in half with sides parallel to each other to create a loop as shown below. Measure up 2″ from the bottom of the loop and sew across both sides of the loop to secure. Set aside.

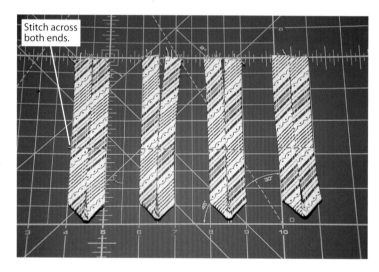

Stitch across both ends.

6. Use a 2½″ Jelly Roll strip and follow the directions on the covered button package to make 4 covered buttons.

7. Center the covered buttons in the middle of each side of the tote and measure down 1½″ from the top edge of the pocket. Sew the buttons in place.

FINISHING

1. Place the tote lining inside the tote with the wrong sides together, making sure you see the right sides of the lining fabric when you look inside the tote bag. Match the 4 corners and ease in the fabric. Pin in place.

2. Baste along the top edge of the tote bag using a ¼″ seam allowance. Take the 4 previously sewn pocket closures and center them in the center of each side of the exterior of the bag. Baste in place.

3. From the long bias strip, cut a piece 2½″ × 45″ to use for the binding along the top edge of the tote. Fold the binding strip in half with wrong sides together and press. Line up the raw edges of the binding along the top edge of the tote and sew using a ⅜″ seam allowance. See Finishing the Binding Ends (page 123) for more information on joining the ends of the binding.

Fold the binding up and over the top of the tote to the inside. Press. Hand stitch or machine stitch the binding in place by stitching in-the-ditch on the exterior of the bag.

Recipe:
Make Life Sewing Kit

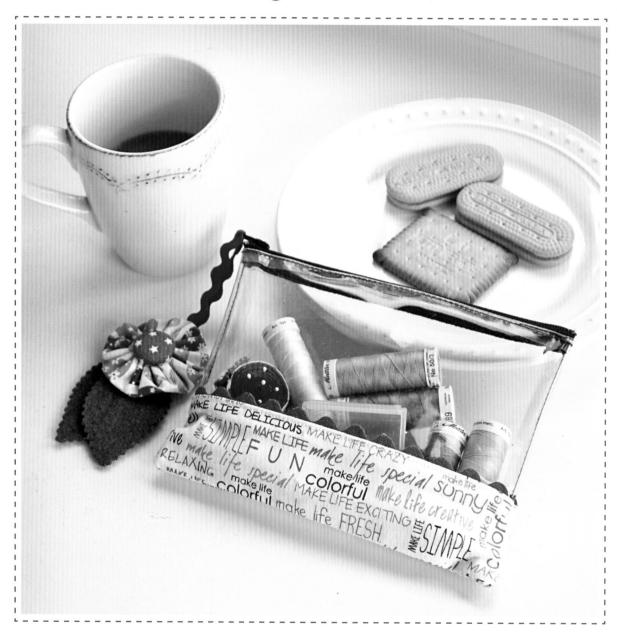

CHEF: Kimberly Walus

YIELD: 1 sewing kit,
finished size 7¼″ × 5″

Make this kit as a stand-alone project or as a companion to the Pack 'N' Go Tote (page 66). Either way, it's a must-have for sewing and quilting projects!

Ingredients

8″ × 8″ clear vinyl

- Cut 2 pieces 4″ × 8″.

1 Jelly Roll strip (I used Make Life by Sweetwater.)

- Cut 4 pieces 2½″ × 8″.

⅛ yard Shape-Flex fusible interfacing

- Cut 2 pieces 2½″ × 8″.

7″ zipper

Garnishes

¾ yard medium (approximately ½″ wide) rickrack for trim and zipper pull

- Cut 2 pieces 8″ long for sewing kit trim.
- Cut 1 piece 8″ long for zipper pull (*optional*).

6″ × 6″ fabric for zipper pull yo-yo (*optional*)

- Cut a 5¼″-diameter circle.

⅞″ covered button for zipper pull (*optional*)

6″ × 6″ green felt for zipper-pull leaves (*optional*)

Instructions

All seam allowances are ¼″ unless otherwise noted.

1. Follow the manufacturer's instructions to fuse the Shape-Flex fusible interfacing pieces to the wrong sides of two 2½″ × 8″ print fabric pieces.

2. Sew an 8″-long piece of rickrack to the top edge of the fused fabric using a ⅛″ seam allowance. Make sure the print is facing in the proper direction as shown. Repeat for the remaining fused fabric.

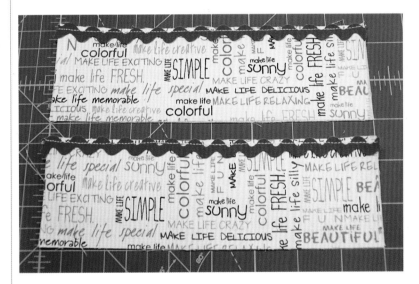

3. Place an 8″ × 4″ piece of vinyl between a 2½″ × 8″ print piece and a 2½″ × 8″ print piece with rickrack. Align the 8″ bottom edges. Be sure the edge with the rickrack is along the bottom and the print pieces are right sides together with the vinyl sandwiched in between.

4. Sew along the bottom 8″ edge using a ¼″ seam allowance. Open and finger press the seam allowances away from the vinyl toward the bottom of the raw fabric edge. Repeat Steps 3 and 4 with the remaining vinyl and print pieces.

5. Topstitch ⅛″ from the fabric/rickrack edge to secure the fabric/rickrack in place. Repeat for the remaining side.

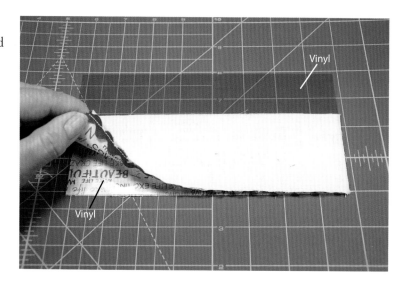

6. With the rickrack piece face up, center the zipper face down along the top edge of the vinyl and pin in place. Place pins ⅛″ from top edge so pinholes will be in the seam allowance. Sew one side of the zipper along the top edge of the vinyl, making sure that the rickrack will end up on the outside of the bag. Repeat for the opposite side.

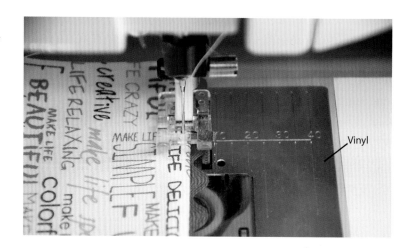

7. Fold the vinyl/zipper seam down toward the bottom of the kit (the vinyl seams will be inside the sewing kit), exposing the zipper. From the right side, flatten the vinyl seam open using a seam roller or your fingers.

8. Topstitch ⅛″ along each edge of the zipper.

9. With the rickrack sides facing each other (rickrack will be on the inside of bag), match where the fabric side seams and the vinyl side seams meet, making sure that the zipper is unzipped before you sew the side seams. This will allow you to turn the bag right side out after sewing it together.

10. Sew the 2 side seams and the bottom seam using a ⅜″ seam allowance. Zigzag the raw edges of fabric seam allowances but not on the vinyl seam allowances. Clip the 2 bottom corners and the 2 zippered corners; then turn the sewing kit right side out.

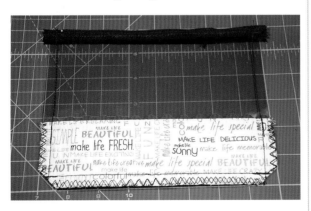

OPTIONAL ZIPPER PULL

1. Make a yo-yo by sewing a running stitch around the outside edge of a 5¼″ circle. Pull the thread to gather the circle into a yo-yo. Knot the thread.

2. Follow manufacturer's directions to cover the button with a scrap of coordinating fabric.

3. Cut 2 leaf shapes from the green felt. Use pinking shears for a serrated edge.

4. Stitch the leaves to the back of the yo-yo, using the project photo (below) for guidance.

5. Stitch the covered button to the center of the yo-yo. Tack the leaves to the back of the yo-yo with a few hand stitches.

6. Thread the 8″ length of rickrack through the sewing kit zipper tab. Secure both ends of the rickrack to the back of the yo-yo with hand stitches or fabric glue.

Recipe:
Jewelry Wallet

CHEF: Roslyn Mirrington

YIELD: 1 jewelry wallet, finished size $9^1/_2$″ × $7^1/_2$″ (folded), $9^1/_2$″ × 34″ (unfolded)

Pretty on the outside and practical on the inside, this elegant jewelry wallet boasts features galore for storing rings, necklaces, earrings, bracelets, and more.

Ingredients

1 Honey Bun (I used Luna Notte by 3 Sisters for Moda.)

⅓ yard linen or linen/cotton blend fabric

⅓ yard coordinating print fabric for the inner panel

¼ yard print fabric for the binding (or use 3 Honey Bun strips)

¾ yard 36″-wide lightweight fusible fleece (I used Vilene H630 by Freudenberg.)

Freezer paper

DMC embroidery floss: #642 dark beige gray and #356 medium terra cotta

5 pearl buttons, ½″ diameter

1 button, ⅞″ diameter

Small handful of polyester fill

1 rectangle 12″ × 6″ of heavyweight clear vinyl

1 rectangle 8″ × 2½″ of gray felt

1 yard ribbon ³⁄₁₆″ wide

9½″ length of ⅜″-wide elastic

7″ zipper

Pencil

Wash-away fabric pen

Metal hook from a wooden coat hanger (*optional*)

8½″ length of ¼″-diameter wooden dowel (*optional*)

Instructions

Seam allowances are ¼″ unless otherwise noted.

OUTER PANEL

1. Cut 1 rectangle 9½″ × 34″ each from the linen and print fabrics. Cut 2 rectangles 9½″ × 34″ from the fusible fleece.

2. Lay 1 rectangle of fusible fleece on your ironing board, with the fusible side up. Lay the linen rectangle on the fleece, and fuse. In the same manner, fuse the print fabric rectangle to the second fusible fleece rectangle.

3. From the Honey Bun, choose 9 strips. From each of these strips, cut an 8″ length. Arrange these strips in a pleasing manner. Join the strips along the 8″ sides to yield an 8″ × 9½″ patchwork rectangle. Press the seams to one side.

4. Crosscut this patchwork rectangle into 1 strip 4½″ × 9½″ and 2 strips 1½″ × 9½″. Reserve the 2 strips 1½″ × 9½″ to use for the Hair Clip / Brooch Band (page 83) and the Felt Earring Keeper (page 87).

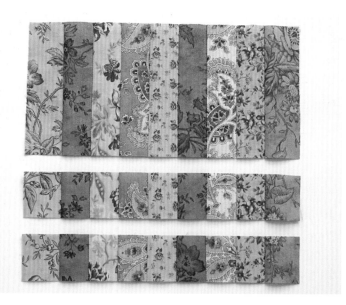

5. Using a sharp lead pencil and a lightbox (or the nearest sunny window), trace the pattern (page 90) onto the dull side of the freezer paper. Cut out on the line.

6. Press the freezer paper template, shiny side down, to the wrong side of the 4½″ × 9½″ patchwork rectangle. Trim the fabric ¼″ outside the wavy edge of the template. Clip the inside curves to within a few threads of the template.

7. Pin the patchwork shape from Step 6 to a 9½″ end of the linen rectangle, keeping the freezer paper template in place. Needle-turn appliqué the patchwork shape to the linen by turning the raw edge under against the freezer paper template. Use tiny stitches in a neutral-colored thread. Remove the freezer paper template.

8. Using the freezer paper template and a wash-away fabric pen, trace 2 wavy lines onto the linen, ¼″ and ¾″ away from the appliquéd edge.

9. Using the line ¼″ away from the appliquéd edge as a guideline, work a row of French knots approximately ¼″ apart using 3 strands of DMC #642. Using 3 strands of DMC #356, work a running stitch along the other traced wavy line, stopping at each peak and valley to secure a pearl button.

10. Cut a 3″ length of ribbon for the button loop. Position the ribbon ends in the center of the patchwork panel, matching the raw edges. Attach to the panel using a ⅛″ seam.

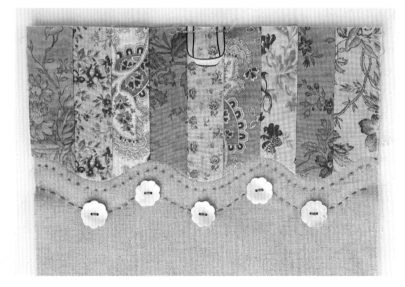

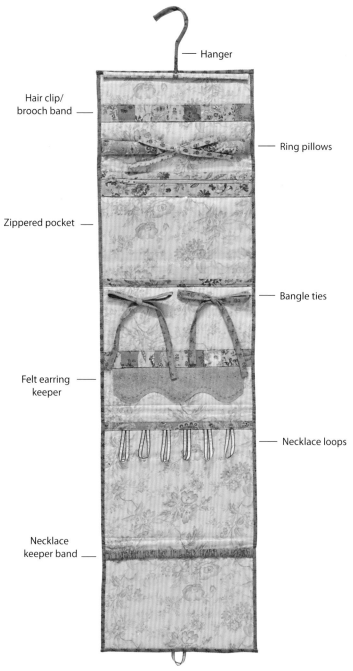

Hanger

Hair clip/ brooch band

Ring pillows

Zippered pocket

Bangle ties

Felt earring keeper

Necklace loops

Necklace keeper band

The wallet unfolds to reveal a complete system for storing necklaces, bracelets, earrings, rings—all your special jewelry.

INNER PANEL

If you want to add a hanger to your jewelry wallet, add the "sleeves" for the wooden dowel at this point. Finish and attach the hanger as part of the final wallet assembly (page 89).

Hanger Sleeves (*optional*)

These narrow fabric channels will accommodate a thin wooden dowel to which you will attach a coat hanger hook.

1. From a Honey Bun strip, cut 2 lengths 1½" × 5¼". Form a double hem on each short end of these lengths by turning the ends to the wrong side of fabric by ¼" and again by ¼". Topstitch this double hem in place. Press each strip in half lengthwise with wrong sides together.

2. Pin hanger sleeves ⅛" from either side of the center, matching the raw edges. Attach to the top edge of the panel using a ⅛" seam.

Covered Hanger Hook (*optional*)

Cut a 1½″ × 6″ length from a Honey Bun strip. Fold in half lengthwise, right sides together. Stitch across one short end. Turn the other short end in by ¼″ to the wrong side of the fabric and press. Turn and fold the strip so that the wrong sides are together. Press. Fold the raw edges in to the pressed center line and press again. Topstitch ⅛″ from the edge along the long sides. Slide the open end of the tube over the coat hanger hook. Set aside.

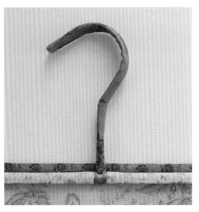

Hair Clip/Brooch Band

1. From a Honey Bun strip, cut a 1½″ × 9½″ strip. Pin this strip, right sides together, to one of the 1½″ × 9½″ patchwork rectangles left from making the outer panel (see Outer Panel, Step 4, page 80). Sew the strips along the 9½″ sides. Turn right side out and press. Topstitch the band ⅛″ from the edge along each 9½″ side.

2. Pin the band 2″ down from the top of the inner panel. Attach it to the side edges of the panel using a ⅛″ seam. Stitch along the seams between the third and fourth patchwork squares and between the sixth and seventh squares, to form 3 sections.

Ring Pillows

Slip your rings over these little "pillows" and tie them securely.

1. To make ties, cut 2 strips 1½″ × 10″ from a Honey Bun strip. For each strip, fold one short end under ¼″ and press. Press in half lengthwise, wrong sides together. Fold the long raw edges in to the pressed center line and press again. Topstitch the ties ⅛″ from the edge along each 10″ side.

2. To make the pillows, cut 4 lengths 1½″ × 5″ from a Honey Bun strip. Sandwich a tie between 2 strips 5″, right sides together. Sew the strips on 3 sides, leaving the tie emerging from the short, open end. Repeat with the remaining 1½″ × 5″ strips.

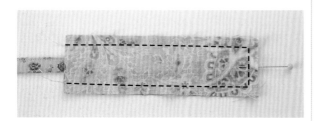

3. Use a coin to mark a semicircle at the closed end of each pillow as a guide for creating a curve.

4. Stitch along the semicircle. Trim the seam to ⅛″ around the curve. Turn each pillow unit right side out and trim to 4″. Fill the pillow lightly with polyester fill. Pin a pillow to either side of the inner panel, 4″ from the top. Attach a pillow to each side edge of the panel using a ⅛″ seam. Form a bow with the ties.

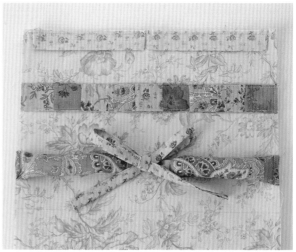

Zippered Pocket

1. From a Honey Bun strip, cut 2 strips 1½″ × 4″. From a second strip, cut 4 lengths 1½″ × 9½″.

2. Fold the 1½″ × 4″ strips in half (so the short ends meet) with the wrong sides together and press. Place the folded strip on 1 end of the 7" zipper. Open the folded strip and stitch it to the zipper along the crease. Fold the strip closed again. Repeat for the opposite end of the zipper. Trim this zipper unit to 9½″.

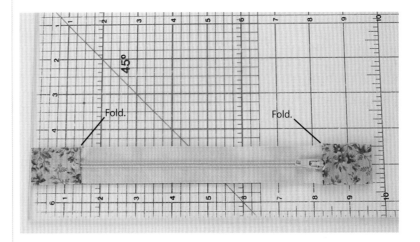

3. Place a 1½″ × 9½″ strip on the zipper unit, right sides together. Turn over so the the wrong side of the zipper is face up. Using a zipper foot, stitch close to the zipper teeth.

4. Repeat Step 3 for the opposite side of the zipper. Press the seams open.

5. Pin another 1½″ × 9½″ strip to the zipper with the right side of the fabric facing the wrong side of the zipper. With the right side of the zipper facing up, sew exactly along the previous row of stitching, close to the zipper teeth. Press the fabric away from the zipper teeth. The wrong side of the zipper unit should now look like the photo on the bottom right.

6. Press the raw edge of each of the 2 lower strips of fabric under ¼″. Slide the 12″ × 6″ rectangle of vinyl between the 2 fabric strips. The vinyl will extend beyond the ends of the zipper.

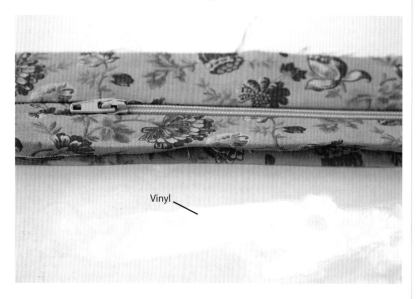

Vinyl

7. Topstitch ⅛″ from the folded edges of the fabric, securing the vinyl in place. Trim the vinyl to measure 9½″ wide and 5″ from the lower edge of the fabric.

8. Press the raw edge of the upper strip of fabric under ¼″. Fold this strip in half toward the zipper and whipstitch the fabric to the previous row of machine stitching along the back side of the zipper.

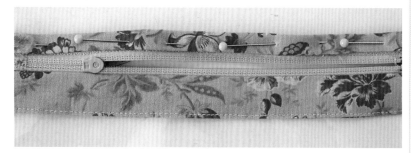

9. To bind the lower edge of the vinyl pocket, sew a 1½″ × 9½″ length of fabric to the bottom edge of the vinyl pocket, right sides together.

> **Tip**
>
> The vinyl is tricky to work with. Keep the vinyl uppermost and the fabric closest to the feed dogs. A walking foot may help with this step.

10. Turn the raw edge of the fabric strip under ¼″ and press. Turn the folded edge to the back of the pocket and whipstitch to the previous row of machine stitching.

11. Pin the top of the zippered pocket 6″ from the top edge of the inner panel. Topstitch the pocket to the panel ⅛″ along the top and bottom edges of the pocket (see the project photo, page 82).

Bangle Ties

1. Cut 2 lengths 1½″ × 20″ from a Honey Bun strip. For each length, turn each short end under ¼″. Press each strip in half lengthwise, wrong sides together. Fold the raw edges in to the pressed center line and press. Fold and press again. Topstitch the ties ⅛″ from the edge along the 20″ sides.

2. Stitch the center of 1 tie to the inner panel, ¾″ below the bottom edge of the zipper pocket, 2½″ in from the left side. Repeat to tack the other tie ¾″ below the pocket and 2½″ from the right side of the panel. See the project photo (page 82) for placement. Tie each tie in a bow.

Felt Earring Keeper

1. Mark a wavy line along one long edge of the 2½″ × 8″ rectangle of felt with a wash-away pen. (You can use the wavy edge of the template pattern, page 90, as a guide.) Cut the felt along this line. Reposition the template and mark another wavy line ¼″ from the cut edge. Work a running stitch along this line with 3 strands of DMC #356.

2. Punch a row of tiny holes 1″ from the top edge of the felt and ½″ apart. You can use a hole punch, nail or a thick needle for this step.

3. From a Honey Bun strip, cut a 1½″ × 9½″ length. With right sides together, pin this length to one of the 1½″ × 9½″ patchwork rectangles left from making the outer panel (see Outer Panel, Step 4, page 80). Sew the strips along the 9½″ sides. Turn right side out and press.

4. Center the felt 17″ down from the top of the panel. Pin the patchwork band over the top edge of the felt and stitch it in place, ⅛″ from the top and bottom edges of the band. See the project photo (page 82) for reference.

Necklace Loops and Keeper Band

Clasp up to six necklaces around these ribbon loops and tuck them under the elasticized band below to keep them untangled.

Necklace Loops

1. Cut a 1½″ × 9½″ length from a Honey Bun strip. Fold it in half, right sides together. Join the long edges of the strip with a ¼″ seam to form a tube. Turn the tube right side out and press.

2. Place a small pencil mark in the center of the band 1½″ from each end. Mark approximately every 1¼″ between the first 2 marks. This will be the back of the band.

3. Cut 6 lengths of ribbon 4½″ long. Using a long machine stitch, baste ribbon loops to the back of the band at each mark. *Note:* This line of stitching will be removed. It keeps the ribbon in place temporarily.

4. Position the band 20½″ from the top of the panel (see the project photo, page 82) and topstitch it in place, ⅛″ from the top and bottom edges of the band. Remove the temporary stitching.

Necklace Keeper Band

1. Cut a 1½″ × 20″ length from a Honey Bun strip. Fold in half lengthwise, right sides together. Stitch the raw edges of the strip with a ¼″ seam to form a tube. Turn the tube right side out and press.

2. Thread a 9½″ length of ⅜″-wide elastic through the tube, gathering the fabric. Stitch across each end of the tube to secure the elastic. Position the band 28″ from the top of the panel and attach it to each side edge of the panel, using a ⅛″ seam. Mark the elasticized band 1¾″ from each end and every 1½″ between the first 2 marks. Machine stitch vertical seams at each mark to form 6 sections.

WALLET ASSEMBLY

1. Place the wrong sides of the outer and inner panels together. *Important:* The decorative section on the outer panel should correspond with the *lower edge* of the inner panel (the section with the necklace keeper band). Stitch the panels together around all 4 sides using a ⅛″ seam.

2. With the inner panel facing up, machine stitch straight rows across the wallet at distances 6″, 12¾″, 19½″, and 27¼″ from the top. The wallet folds along these rows when it is closed.

Binding

1. The edges of the jewelry wallet are bound with a narrow, butted binding. There are 2 options for the binding. For a scrappy look, join 3 Honey Bun strips to yield a 105″ length of binding. Alternatively, for a more uniform look, cut and join 3 strips 1½″ × 45″ from the optional ¼ yard print fabric. Join the binding strips diagonally.

2. Fold the joined strips in half lengthwise, wrong sides together, and press. Cut 2 lengths 34″ from the binding strip. With raw edges together, stitch a strip to the left and right edges of the outer panel of the wallet using a ¼″ seam. Trim the seam allowance to ⅛″. Turn the binding over to the inside of the wallet and whipstitch in place by hand.

3. Cut 2 lengths 10″ from the remaining binding strip. Turn under the short ends of each strip by ¼″. Stitch the strips to the top and bottom edges of the wallet. Trim the seam allowances as before; then fold the binding to the inside of the wallet and stitch it in place.

Hanger Assembly (*optional*)

1. Mark the center of the 8½″ length of wooden dowel. Using a small drill bit the same size as the thread on the coat hanger hook, carefully drill a hole through the center of the dowel.

2. Insert the dowel through the hanging sleeves on the wallet. Screw the coat hanger hook into the dowel.

3. Fasten the fabric hook cover to the dowel using embroidery thread. Catch the fabric hook cover with a stitch, wrap thread around the dowel and catch the fabric again. Repeat several times to secure hook to sleeves.

Button Closure

Fold the wallet closed and determine the button position on the outer panel. Mark this point lightly with pencil, ensuring it is centered on the panel. If using a fabric-covered button, cover according to the manufacturer's instructions. Stitch the button to the outer panel (refer to the photo on page 78).

Your elegant jewelry wallet is ready to use!

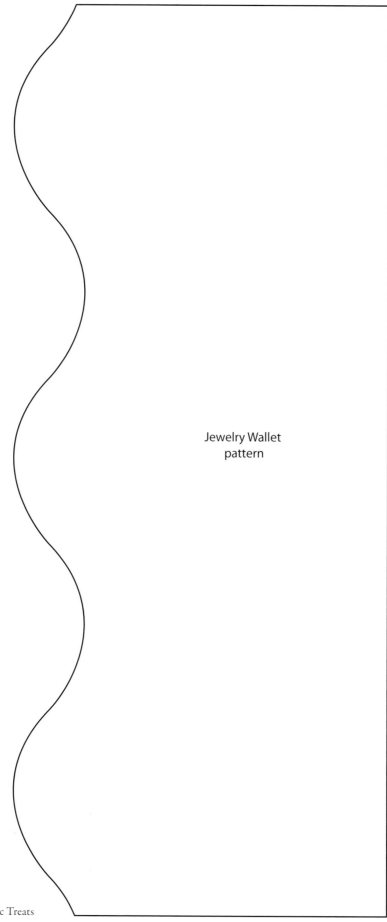

Jewelry Wallet
pattern

Recipe:

Zippity Doodle Bag

CHEF: Jenny Garland

YIELD: 1 bag,
finished size 19″ × 16″ × 6″

The Zippity Doodle Bag is the perfect size for your little one to take on an overnight trip to Grandma's house. It features a recessed zipper and exterior pockets designed to hold fun stuff like a sketch pad and crayons.

Ingredients

Exterior blocks: 9 Layer Cake squares

Exterior sashing and lining: 1 yard fabric (More fabric may be required for directional prints.)

- Cut 6 strips 2″ × 16½″ for vertical sashing.
- Cut 4 strips 2″ × 21″ for horizontal sashing.
- Cut 2 rectangles 21″ × 19½″ for the lining.

Batting: 24″ × 48″ (I used Luna batting by Moda.)

- Cut 2 rectangles 23½″ × 21½″.

Backing: ¾ yard muslin

- Cut 2 rectangles 23½″ × 21½″.

Fusible interfacing: 1¾ yards 44″ wide (I used Décor-Bond by Pellon.)

- Cut 2 rectangles 23½″ × 21½″ for the bag exterior.
- Cut 1 rectangle 14″ × 5″ for the pocket.
- Cut 2 rectangles 4″ × 18″ for the straps.
- Cut 2 rectangles 21″ × 19½″ for the lining.

Pocket and straps: ⅓ yard accent fabric

- Cut 1 rectangle 14″ × 5″ for the exterior pocket.
- Cut 1 rectangle 14″ × 5″ for the pocket lining.
- Cut 2 rectangles 4″ × 18″ for the straps.

18″ zipper

Instructions

Unless otherwise noted, seam allowances are ¼″.

BLOCK ASSEMBLY

1. Stack 9 Layer Cake squares right side up, aligning the raw edges. Cut an angle 2″ in from the bottom right to 3″ in from the top right.

2. Move 1 top small piece and place it right side up on the bottom of the stack.

3. Sew each small and large piece right sides together. Press. Keep the blocks in order.

4. Stack the blocks neatly. Cut an angle 2″ in from the bottom left to 4″ in from the top left.

5. Move 2 top small pieces and place them right side up on the bottom of the stack.

6. Sew each small and large piece right sides together. Press. Keep the blocks in order.

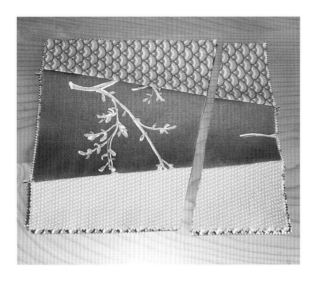

7. Stack the blocks neatly again. Turn the stack 90° and cut an angle 4″ in from the bottom right to 2″ in from the top right.

8. Move the top 3 small pieces and place them right side up on the bottom of the stack. Sew each small and large piece right sides together. Press. Keep the blocks in order.

9. Restack the blocks. Cut an angle 3″ in from the bottom left to 2″ in from the top left. Move 6 top small pieces and place them right side up on the bottom of the stack. Sew each small and large piece right sides together. Press. Trim each block to 8½″ × 8½″.

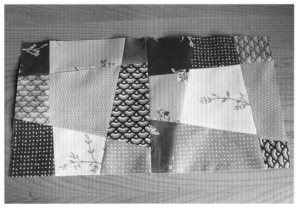

10. Set aside 1 block (you will not need it). Sew 2 blocks right sides together along one edge. Press. Repeat with the remaining 6 blocks to create 4 sets of 2 blocks.

EXTERIOR PANEL

1. Sew a 2″ × 16½″ vertical sashing strip between 2 sets of 2 Nine Patch blocks. Add a vertical sashing strip to either side of the panel. Repeat for the second exterior panel.

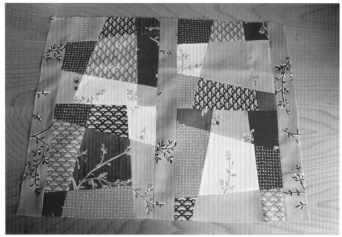

2. Sew a 2″ × 21″ horizontal sashing strip to the top and bottom of each exterior panel.

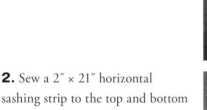

3. Fuse a 23½″ × 21½″ interfacing rectangle to the wrong side of each 23½″ × 21½″ muslin rectangle.

4. Place the 23½″ × 21½″ fused muslin right side down on a table. Place a 23½″ × 21½″ piece of batting on top of the fused muslin. Center 1 exterior panel right side up on top of the batting. Baste and quilt as desired. Trim the batting and muslin to align with the raw edges of the exterior panel.

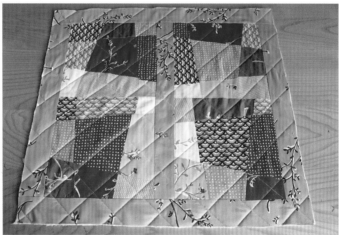

5. Repeat Steps 1–4 to create another exterior panel.

POCKET

1. Fuse the 14″ × 5″ interfacing to the wrong side of the exterior pocket fabric.

2. Layer the fused exterior pocket fabric with the pocket lining, right sides together. Stitch around the perimeter, leaving a 6″ opening at the bottom for turning. Clip the corners, turn right side out, and press. Edge stitch the top of the pocket with ⅛″ and ¼″ seams.

3. Measure 9″ down from the center of the top edge of an exterior panel. Center the top edge of the pocket at this point and pin the pocket in place. Stitch the sides and bottom of the pocket to the exterior panel.

4. Divide the pocket with vertical seams as desired. The bag pictured has one 7¼″ section and six 1″ sections (see project photo, page 92).

STRAPS

1. Fuse a 4″ × 18″ interfacing rectangle to the wrong side of each 4″ × 18″ strap rectangle.

2. Fold a strap in half lengthwise, wrong sides together, and press. Open. Fold the raw edges to meet the pressed line and press. Fold again and press. Topstitch ⅛″ along each long side. Stitch ¼″ in from each topstitched line. Repeat Steps 1 and 2 with the other strap.

LINING AND RECESSED ZIPPER

1. Fuse a 21″ × 19½″ interfacing rectangle to the wrong side of each 21″ × 19½″ lining fabric.

2. Cut a horizontal line 2½″ from the top edge (21″) of each fused rectangle. You will have 2 rectangles measuring 21″ × 2½″ and 2 rectangles measuring 21″ × 17″.

3. Center and pin the zipper to a 21″ × 2½″ rectangle, right sides together, aligning the raw fabric edge with one edge of the zipper tape. Sew it in place with a zipper foot.

Tip

As you get close to the zipper pull, lower your needle, raise the presser foot, and slide the zipper pull to the other side of the needle. Resume sewing.

4. With right sides together, pin the zipper edge of the 21″ × 2½″ rectangle from Step 3 to a 21″ × 17″ rectangle from Step 2, aligning the raw edges. The right sides of the fabric face each other with the zipper sandwiched in between.

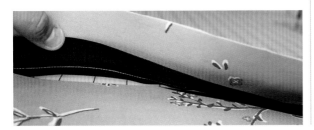

5. Sew in place with a zipper foot on top of the previous stitching. Repeat Steps 3–5 to attach the other side of the zipper to the remaining 21″ × 2½″ and 21″ × 17″ rectangles.

FINAL ASSEMBLY

1. Pin 1 strap to the right side of each exterior panel, measuring 7″ in from each side of the 21″ top edge. Baste the straps in place.

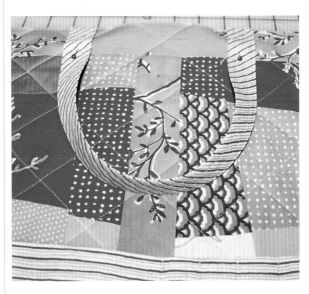

2. Open the zipper halfway. Pin 1 exterior panel to 1 lining panel, right sides together, along the top edge.

3. Stitch a ½″ seam allowance along the top edge.

4. Repeat Steps 2–3 with the remaining exterior and lining panel.

5. Pin the exterior panels and the lining panels right sides together so the front and back exterior panels face each other and the front and back linings face each other. Stitch the sides and bottom with a ½″ seam allowance, getting as close as possible to the zipper ends. Leave an 8″ opening on the lining side for turning. Clip thick areas in the seam allowance to reduce bulk.

6. Pinch each exterior and lining corner seam on the bottom and side, matching seams in the middle. Pin through all thicknesses and measure 2½″ from the corner point. Draw a horizontal line and stitch to form a gusset.

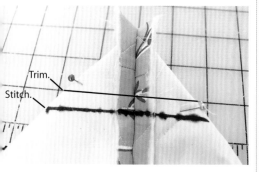

7. Trim the corner seam, leaving a ½″ seam allowance.

8. Pull the bag right side out through the opening in the lining and slipstitch the opening to close. Topstitch the top edge of the bag under the straps.

Recipe:
"Shirt Off My Bag" Tiny Tote Bag

CHEF: Monica Solorio-Snow

YIELD: 1 bag,
finished size 5½″ × 8½″ × 2″

Tiny "shirt front" totes can hold anything from sewing notions to cosmetics. Make them in all your favorite fabrics to give or to use.

Ingredients

5 Layer Cake "slices" (10″ × 10″ pieces)

Slice A:

- Cut 2 squares 5″ × 5″ for the prairie points collar.

- Cut 2 strips 2″ × 10″ for the handles.

Slices B, C, and D:

- From each print, cut 2 rectangles 8″ × 10″ for the lining (B and C) and 1 rectangle 8″ × 10″ for the back (D).

Slice E:

- Square up to 10″ × 10″, if necessary, for the shirt front.

Garnish

5 buttons ½″ diameter for embellishment

Instructions

Note: All seam allowances are ¼″ unless noted.

BAG "SHIRT" FRONT

1. Fold slice E at the center (do not make a crease). Draw a line with your favorite marking tool, 1″ from the fold.

2. Stitch along the marked line to form a tube.

3. Press flat at the center of the tube to form the center placket (the double layer of fabric that holds the buttons).

4. From the top of the placket, mark on the center every 1″ for the 5 buttons. Sew the buttons in place.

COLLAR AND STRAPS

1. Make a prairie point by folding a 5″ × 5″ square diagonally with the wrong sides together and press. Fold diagonally again and press. Make 2.

2. Align the top raw edge of the prairie point with the top edge of the "shirt" (E). Overlap prairie points above placket. Pin in place.

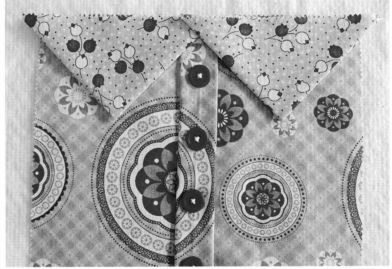

3. Fold a 2″ × 10″ A strip in half lengthwise, with wrong sides together. Open and press the long edges to the center. Refold in half lengthwise and press to form the handle. Make 2.

4. Topstitch on the outer edges (as close to the edge as possible) on each handle strap.

5. Align the handle strap's raw edges to the shirt top raw edge, 1¾" from each side. Pin.

6. Baste with a ⅛" seam allowance to hold the prairie points and handle strap in place. Trim the corners of the prairie points that extend beyond the side of the shirt front (E).

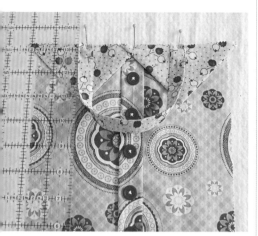

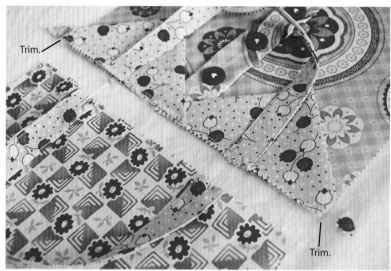

7. Repeat Steps 5 and 6 to attach the remaining handle to the back D fabric.

BAG ASSEMBLY

1. Layer the D unit with a lining B unit, and layer an E unit with a lining C unit with right sides together. Pin. Join with a seam across the top for each set.

3. Layer each unit, right sides together—front and back pieces (E and D) right sides together, and lining pieces (B and C) right sides together. Pin.

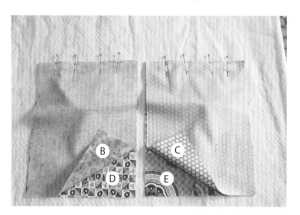

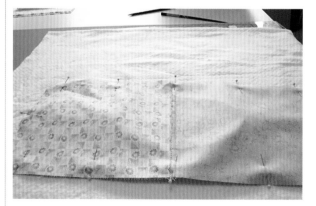

2. Press the DB seam to the back (D). Press the EC seam to the lining (C).

4. Stitch completely around all 4 sides, leaving a 3″ opening centered at the bottom of lining B/C for turning.

5. To create boxed corners in the bag, pinch each corner so that the front and back seams align vertically—creating a triangle. Mark a line 1″ from the point. Stitch on the line with a backstitch at both ends to lock the stitch. Trim off the bulky triangle ends. Repeat for lining corners.

6. Turn the bag right side out. Pin the opening and edgestitch closed.

7. Tuck the lining inside the bag and press. Done!

Recipe:

The September Bag, Laptop Sleeve, and Storage Pouch

CHEF: Melissa Mortenson

YIELD: 1 September bag, 1 laptop sleeve, and 1 storage pouch

Carry your "desk" with you in style with these bright and practical accessories. Separate pieces for your laptop and accessories all stow neatly away and stay protected inside the large shoulder bag. There's even room for your notebooks and paper files.

Fabric Tips

You can make all 3 of these coordinating pieces from 1 Fat Quarter Bundle (as many as 40 pieces) and 1 Jelly Roll (40 strips). Even though you will only need 20 fat quarters to complete these 3 projects, it's nice to buy the Fat Quarter Bundle so you can be confident all the fabrics will work together. The instructions assume you will use 1 fat quarter per piece. You can save leftovers for another project, or you could use the scraps for other parts of this project instead.

Before you begin, identify which fat quarters you wish to use for each bag. You may want to match colors, prints, or patterns; for example, you may want to use all your red pieces on the outside of the bag and all your aqua pieces on your laptop sleeve.

Think about how you want the fabric pattern to lie on each bag and cut your fat quarters accordingly. For example, if you are cutting a striped fat quarter, do you want the stripes to go horizontally or vertically across the bag?

September Bag

YIELD: 1 September bag, finished size 16″ × 11″ × 4″

This roomy bag has a lining with two pockets, an adjustable button strap closure, and even a ribbon for attaching your keys.

Ingredients

Exterior and lining: 13 fat quarters (Each piece is cut from a separate fat quarter unless otherwise noted.)

- Cut 6 pieces 17″ × 12″ for the front, back, lining front, lining back, flap front (save the remaining fat quarter fabric to cut your front stripe piece), and flap lining.

- Cut 2 pieces 17″ × 8″ for the pocket and pocket lining.

- Cut 2 pieces 14″ × 9″ for the zippered pocket and zippered pocket lining.

- Cut 1 piece 8″ × 18″ for the bottom reinforcement piece.

- Cut 1 piece 6″ × 12″ for the front stripe (use reserved fabric from the flap front piece).

- Use 1 fat quarter for the lettering on all 3 projects.

Gusset, flap stripes, and strap:
13 Jelly Roll strips

- Cut 4 Jelly Roll strips 41″ long for the gusset and gusset lining.

- Cut 3 Jelly Roll strips 13″ long for stripes on the flap front.

- Select 4 uncut Jelly Roll Strips for the strap and strap lining.

- Using 2 Jelly Roll strips, cut 4 strips 2½″ × 12″ long for the ring strap and ring strap lining.

Fusible fleece: ¾ yard 44″ wide

- Cut 3 pieces 17″ × 12″ for the flap, front, and back.

- Cut 1 piece 4½″ × 41″ for the gusset.

Fusible interfacing (heavyweight): 2 yards 44″ wide (I used Décor-Bond by Pellon.)

- Cut 6 pieces 17″ × 12″ for the flap, flap lining, lining (2), front, and back.

- Cut 2 pieces 4½″ × 41″ for the gusset.

- Cut 1 piece 4½″ × 44″ for the strap.

- Cut 1 piece 17″ × 8″ for the pocket.

- Cut 1 piece 2″ × 2″ for the magnetic closure.

- Cut 1 piece 4½″ × 12″ for the ring strap.

Extra supplies:

9″ zipper

2″ metal ring (available at most hardware stores)

Fusible web: 17″ × 36″ for lettering (I used HeatnBond Lite.)

Garnishes

12 buttons 1″ diameter

1 carabiner clip (available at most hardware stores)

12″ ribbon ½″ wide to attach carabiner clip

Heavy-duty thread

Magnetic snap (If you're concerned that a magnetic closure might affect your credit cards or computer, use a traditional snap or button instead.)

3½″ × 15″ piece of heavy plastic canvas (Smaller pieces of plastic canvas can be pieced together with duct tape; it won't show.)

Water-soluble fabric pen

Instructions

All seams are ½″ unless otherwise noted.

BAG FLAP

1. Using a ¼″ seam, sew the 3 Jelly Roll strips 2½″ × 13″ together along the long sides. Press the seams open. Turn under the 13″ raw edges ¼″ and press.

> **Tip**
>
> If you have trouble turning the edges under, you can use a bit of quilt basting spray to help the edges lie flat while you press them.

2. Pin the assembled Jelly Roll strips to the bag flap front 2″ in from the left side of the flap. Pin well and stitch to the flap by sewing close to each folded edge of the Jelly Roll unit. Topstitch each Jelly Roll strip ⅛″ from the seam on both sides.

3. Trim the edges of the Jelly Roll unit even with the bag flap front piece. Using a soup can or other round object, trace the curve of the can onto the bottom 2 corners of the bag flap and bag flap lining to create rounded corners. Trim.

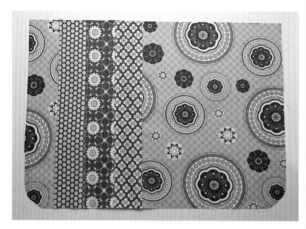

4. Using a word processing program, print the word *tote* in Arial Black font at 275 points. Using a lightbox, place the printed word face down and trace the letters onto the paper side of a piece of fusible web. The letters will be traced backward. Loosely cut around each letter. Place the rough side of the fusible web down on the wrong side of a fat quarter and fuse with an iron.

5. Cut out each letter. Arrange the letters on the bottom right side of the bag flap piece 1″ from the bottom of the flap and 1½″ in from the right side of the bag flap. Use a ruler to make sure that the letters are lined up properly. Iron the letters in place. Stitch around the outline of each letter close to the edge. Go slowly and pivot with the needle down when needed.

6. Fuse a 17″ × 12″ piece of fusible fleece to the wrong side of the bag flap. Trim to match the rounded corners. Fuse a 17″ × 12″ piece of heavy-weight fusible interfacing on top of the fusible fleece. Trim to match the rounded corners. Set the bag flap front piece aside.

7. Fuse a 17″ × 12″ piece of heavyweight fusible interfacing to the wrong side of your bag flap lining piece. Trim to match the rounded corners. Measure up 2″ from the bottom of the bag flap lining piece and in 8½″ from the side. Mark this location with an X using a water-soluble fabric pen.

8. Place the 2″ × 2″ square of heavyweight interfacing on the mark you just made and iron it onto the wrong side of the flap lining piece (this is reinforcement for the magnetic snap). Attach the female side of the magnetic snap to the center of the 2″ square following the manufacturer's directions.

9. Place the bag flap piece and bag flap lining piece right sides together. Pin well. Stitch around 3 sides of the bag flap piece, leaving the top seam open. Clip the curves. Turn right side out and press well. Topstitch the bag flap close to the edge on 3 sides. Set the bag flap aside.

BAG LINING

1. Iron a piece of 17″ × 12″ fusible heavyweight interfacing onto the wrong side of one of your bag lining pieces. This will be the front bag lining. Using a water-soluble fabric pen, draw a 9″ line, 3″ from the top edge of the bag lining piece, parallel to the top edge and centered side to side.

2. Pin one of the 14″ × 9″ zipper pocket pieces to the back of the bag lining piece, wrong sides together. Center the zippered pocket piece on the bag lining piece.

3. Cut along the 9″ line you just drew, *through both layers of fabric.* At each end of the cut line, cut a ¼″ slit at a 45° angle from the cut line. Fold the fabric under ¼″ along the top and bottom sides of your cut line. Press well. Fold under the 2 triangular-shaped pieces of fabric along the 2 short sides of your cut opening. Press well.

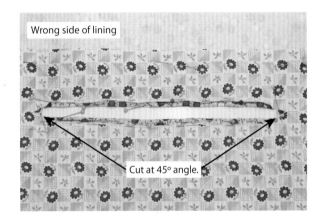

Wrong side of lining

Cut at 45º angle.

4. Pin the zipper into the opening you just formed. Using a zipper foot on your machine, topstitch around all 4 sides of the zipper.

5. Take the other 14″ × 9″ zipper pocket piece and pin it to the first zipper pocket piece, right sides together. Stitch around all 4 sides of the pocket without stitching through the lining piece. Set aside.

6. Fuse heavyweight fusible interfacing onto the wrong side of the remaining 17″ × 12″ lining piece. This is the back lining.

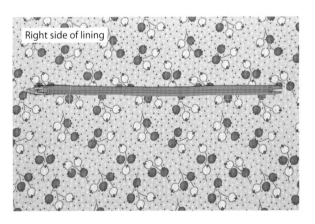

Right side of lining

7. Fuse interfacing to the wrong side of one of the 17″ × 8″ pocket pieces. With right sides together, sew the interfaced 17″ × 8″ pocket piece to the other 17″ × 8″ pocket piece along a 17″ edge. Press the seam open. Turn right side out. Press and topstitch the sewn edge.

8. Pin the pocket piece to the bag lining piece, matching side and bottom edges. Baste along bottom and sides.

9. Measure in 5″ from each side of the pocket and draw a straight line parallel to the side with your erasable fabric pen. Stitch on the drawn lines to divide the pocket. Begin stitching at the bottom of the pocket and make sure you backstitch several times when you get to the top. Set the bag lining piece aside.

10. Using a ¼″ seam, stitch 2 Jelly Roll strips 41″ long together along the long edges, to form the bag lining gusset. Press the seam open. Fuse a 4½″ × 41″ piece of heavy-weight fusible interfacing to the wrong side of the Jelly Roll strips.

11. Pin 1 bag gusset lining to the front bag lining piece, right sides together, along 3 sides (2 sides and bottom). Pinch the gusset lining piece at the corners so that it will lie flat when you are sewing around the corners. Stitch. Trim any extra bag gusset lining flush with the bag lining piece along the top edge.

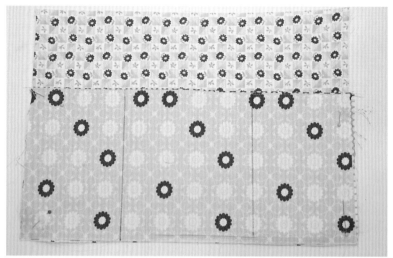

Back lining

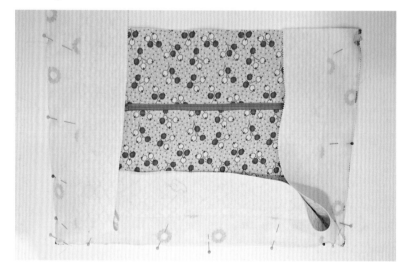

Front lining and gusset

12. Pin one end of the 12″-long piece of ribbon along one side edge of the back bag lining piece, 2″ down from the top. Stitch in place close to the edge. The carabiner clip will be attached to the loose end of the ribbon in the Finishing section, Step 1 (page 113).

13. Repeat Step 11 to attach the bag gusset lining to the back bag lining piece. Press the seams open. Turn right side out. Set aside.

BAG EXTERIOR

1. Press each 12″ side of the 6″ × 12″ bag stripe piece under ¼″. Place on top of the bag front piece 2″ in from the left side. Topstitch along each folded edge to attach the stripe to the bag front piece.

2. Fuse fusible fleece to the wrong side of both bag front and bag back pieces. Fuse heavyweight fusible interfacing on top of the fusible fleece.

3. Stitch the 2 gusset Jelly Roll pieces together along the 41″ side with a ¼″ seam. Press the seam open. Apply the 4½″ × 41″ piece of fusible fleece to the wrong side of the gusset piece. Fuse heavyweight fusible interfacing to the back of the fusible fleece.

4. Attach the bag gusset to the bag front and back piece as outlined in Step 11 for the bag lining (page 110). Press the seams open.

5. Pin the bag flap to the top of the bag back piece, right sides together. Stitch in place with a ¼″ seam.

6. Apply the male section of the magnetic snap to the bag front piece, centered 6″ from the top edge, following the manufacturer's directions.

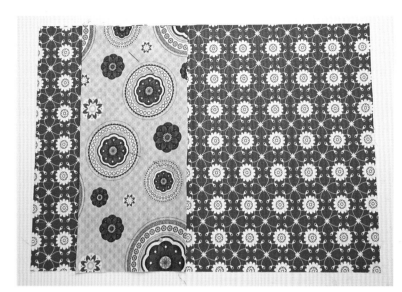

STRAP

1. To make the strap, sew 2 uncut Jelly Roll strips together along the long edge using a ¼″ seam allowance. Press the seam open. Repeat with 2 additional uncut Jelly Roll strips to create the strap lining piece. Apply a 4½″ × 44″ piece of heavyweight fusible interfacing to the wrong side of the strap.

2. Place the strap and strap lining pieces right sides together. Using a ¼″ seam allowance, sew along 1 short and 2 long sides of the strap. Trim the corners. Turn right side out and press. Topstitch along the 3 sewn edges of the strap.

3. Sew 2 ring strap pieces 2½″ × 12″ together along the 12″ edge with a ¼″ seam allowance. Press the seam open. Repeat for 2 ring strap lining pieces. Iron a 4½″ × 12″ piece of heavyweight fusible interfacing to the wrong side of the ring strap piece. Place the ring strap piece and the ring strap lining piece right sides together. Using a ¼″ seam allowance, stitch along the 2 long edges. Turn right side out and press. Topstitch along the sewn edges.

4. Feed the ring strap piece through a 2″ metal ring. Match the raw edges and baste.

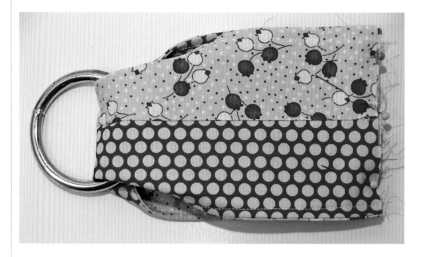

5. Pin the ring strap piece to the bag on one side at the gusset, right sides together, matching the raw edges. Stitch in place. Repeat stitching to reinforce the seam.

6. Pin the strap to the bag at the gusset on the opposite side, right sides together, matching the raw edges. Stitch in place. Repeat stitching to reinforce the seam.

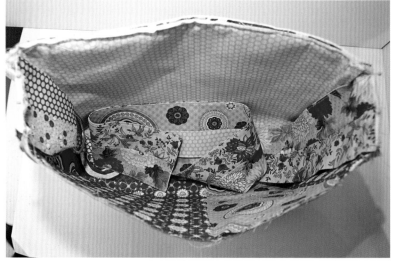

BAG ASSEMBLY

1. With the bag inside out and bag lining right side out, slip the bag lining into the bag. Make sure that the 2 pieces line up at each of the seams. If they don't, remove the bag lining piece and adjust the seams as necessary. Pin the bag to the bag lining in several places along the upper edge.

2. Begin stitching 1″ from the bag/bag gusset seam on the bag front, stitching toward the gusset. Continue stitching around the bag, stitching the bag back and then the other bag gusset, stopping 1″ past the bag/bag gusset seam on the opposite side. You may find it helpful to take off the removable part of the bed of your sewing machine during this step. Turn the bag right side out using the opening you just left in the bag. Press very well.

3. Turn under the open seam at the bag front and press. Beginning at the bag back/bag gusset seam, topstitch the top edge of the bag. You will topstitch the bag gusset, bag front (closing the opening as you sew), and the other bag gusset. You will not topstitch the bag back.

FINISHING

1. Fold under the raw edge of the ribbon that is attached to the bag lining ⅛″ and stitch. Fold under again, this time ½″, and stitch, making sure to backstitch. Feed the carabiner ring through the loop you just made in the ribbon.

2. Mark then stitch 2 buttonholes in the end of the strap, 1½″ from the end of the strap, and centered in each Jelly Roll strip.

3. Mark the strap in both Jelly Roll strips at 14″, 16″, and 18″ from the end of the strap. Using heavy-duty thread, stitch 2 buttons to each spot you just marked, with 1 button on the top of the strap and 1 button on the back of the strap. (Using an additional button on the back will reinforce the top button so it will not pop off with the weight of the bag.)

> **Tip**
>
> While sewing the button, place a bamboo skewer or 2 toothpicks under the button. This will give the buttons some slack for ease in use.

4. To make the reinforcing strip for the inside bag bottom, take your 8″ × 18″ piece of fabric and fold it in half lengthwise. Stitch around 3 sides, leaving 1 short end open. Clip the corners and turn it right side out and press.

5. Slip the 3½″ × 15″ piece of plastic canvas into this piece. Fold in and turn under the raw edge and press. Topstitch closed. Slip the piece into the bag bottom. You can stitch the corners in place if you like, but I just left mine loose.

Laptop Sleeve

A lining of soft fleece and upholstery foam gives your laptop maximum cushioning in this pretty sleeve.

Tip

This sleeve is made to fit a laptop measuring 14½" × 10" and 1" thick. If your laptop is larger, measure it and cut your sleeve pieces as follows. For the sleeve front and back, add 1½" to your laptop's length and 2½" to its width. If your laptop is more than 1" thick, add the difference between its thickness and 1" to the width × 2. Adjust your sleeve flap size accordingly.

Note: The larger you make the laptop sleeve, the more likely it is that it may not fit in the September bag. Remember: a fat quarter piece is 18" × 22"; if your sleeve front and back pieces are larger than that, you will need to use yardage instead of fat quarters.

Garnishes

Ties: 1 yard ribbon ½" wide

- Cut 2 pieces each 16" long.

Ingredients

Exterior panels and flap: 4 fat quarters

- Cut 2 pieces 16½" × 12½" for the front and back.

- Cut 2 pieces 7" × 12" for the flap front and flap front lining.

Lettering: 1 fat quarter (You can use the same fat quarter you used for the lettering on the September bag.)

Stripes and handle: 3 Jelly Roll strips

- Cut 2 Jelly Roll strips 16½" long for the front stripes.

- Cut 1 Jelly Roll strip 9" long for the handle.

Fleece lining: ½ yard Moda Snuggles fabric

- Cut 2 pieces 16" × 12½".

Foam: ½ yard ¼"-thick upholstery foam (If you can't find this at a fabric store, try an auto upholstery shop.)

- Cut 2 pieces 16" × 12½" for the front and back.

- Cut 1 piece 7" × 12" for the flap.

Heavyweight fusible interfacing (*optional*)

- Cut 1 piece 4½" × 16½" for the front stripes.

Fusible web: ⅛ yard for lettering

Instructions

1. Sew together 2 Jelly Roll strips 2½″ × 16½″ along the long edges with a ¼″ seam allowance for the front stripe. Press the seam open.

Note: If your Jelly Roll pieces are lighter than the main fabric on your laptop sleeve and the darker fabric of the laptop sleeve may show through the Jelly Roll strips, apply a 4½″ × 16½″ piece of heavy-weight fusible interfacing to the wrong side of your sewn Jelly Roll pieces. If the main fabric will not show through the Jelly Roll pieces, you can skip this step.

2. Turn under the raw edges ¼″ and press.

3. Print the word *type* in Arial Black font at 250 points. Trace and cut out the letters as outlined for the September bag construction (see Bag Flap, Step 4, page 108).

4. Place letters on the assembled Jelly Roll strips, 2″ in from the right side. Press in place and stitch around each letter.

5. Place the Jelly Roll strip on the sleeve front piece 1″ from the bottom of the sleeve front piece. Topstitch along the top and bottom edges of the Jelly Roll piece to attach it to the sleeve front piece. Trim the entire piece to 16″ × 12½″.

6. To create the handle, fold the 2½″ × 9″ Jelly Roll strip in half lengthwise, with right sides together. Stitch along the 9″ edge, using a ¼″ seam. Turn right side out and place the seam in the center of strip. Press well. Topstitch along both long sides. Fold in half, matching the raw edges, and pin to the top left corner of the sleeve front piece, 2″ in from the left side as shown in the photo below. Stitch in place.

7. Take a 16″ piece of ribbon and pin it to the sleeve front piece 6″ in from the left side of the sleeve and 6¼″ from the top of the piece. Fold under raw end ¼″ and stitch close to the folded edge of the ribbon.

8. Fold the ribbon over and stitch again, ½″ from where you stitched previously. The ribbon should now be lying toward the left side of the sleeve front piece.

9. Using the same can you used to curve the corners of the laptop bag flap (Step 3, page 108), curve the top and bottom right-hand corners of the 12½″ × 6½″ sleeve front, sleeve back, 2 upholstery foam pieces, and 2 Snuggles pieces.

10. Place your sleeve front and sleeve back pieces right sides together. Place your 2 foam pieces 12½″ × 16″ on top of the sleeve front and under the sleeve back. Stitch the pieces together leaving the left side open. Clip the curves.

11. Sew 2 Snuggles pieces, right sides together, leaving the left straight side open. Clip the seams and turn right side out.

12. Cut a curve on the top and bottom right corners of the flap front, flap lining, and flap upholstery foam pieces.

13. Stitch the other 16″-long ribbon piece to the flap front at the center with the ribbon edge flush with the curved edge of the flap. (See bottom photo, page 117, for reference.)

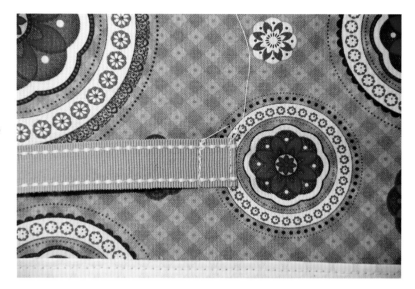

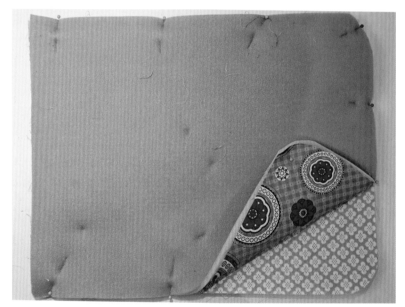

14. Place the flap front and flap lining pieces right side together. Place the upholstery foam piece on top of the wrong side of the flap front piece. Pin well. Stitch around the flap, leaving the straight edge open. Clip the curves, turn right side out, and press. Topstitch the flap close to the edge.

15. Pin the flap to the sleeve back piece with right sides together. Stitch.

16. Place a Snuggles lining piece inside the sleeve with right sides together. Your lining piece will be right side out, and your sleeve will be wrong side out. Line up the seams exactly. If they are not exact, adjust the seams of the sleeve lining piece until they line up properly. Pin around the entire opening, matching seams and centers.

17. Stitch, beginning 1″ from the front/back seam around the back of the sleeve and stopping 1″ beyond the opposite front/back seam. You will have an opening approximately 9″ wide on the front.

18. Turn the sleeve right side out through the opening and press. Fold under the edges of the opening and pin. Topstitch to close the opening. Do not topstitch the sleeve back.

Zippered Storage Pouch

YIELD: 1 pouch, finished size 12″ × 8″

Use this little pouch for your computer cord.

Ingredients

Exterior and lining: 2 fat quarters

- Cut 1 fat quarter into 2 pieces, each 13″ × 9″ for the front and back.

- Cut 1 fat quarter into 2 pieces, each 13″ × 9″ for the lining.

Ruffle: 1 Jelly Roll strip

- Cut 1 strip 2½″ × 18″.

12″ zipper

Fusible web: ⅛ yard for lettering

Lettering: 1 fat quarter (You can use the same fat quarter that you used for the lettering on the bag and sleeve.)

Garnishes

Gathering foot for the sewing machine (*optional*)

Instructions

1. Print the word *store* in Arial Black font at 225 points. Trace and cut out the letters as outlined for the laptop bag construction (see Bag Flap, Step 4, page 108). Fuse the letters onto the pouch front piece 1″ up from the bottom and 1″ in from the right edge. Stitch around the outline of all the letters.

2. Using your gathering foot, gather the 18″-long Jelly Roll strip piece down the middle. If you do not have a gathering foot, run a basting stitch down the center of the Jelly Roll strip and pull up on the threads to gather it, so the gathered strip measures approximately 9″ long.

3. Pin the gathered Jelly Roll strip to the pouch front, 2″ from the left edge. Stitch down the middle of the ruffle on top of your previous stitching to secure it to the pouch front. Trim the ruffle ends even with the top and bottom of the pouch.

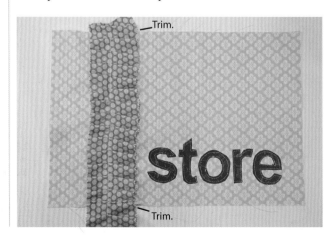

Trim.

Trim.

4. Pin the top of the zipper to the right side of the front. Pin the right side of the lining piece to the back of the zipper. Your pouch front and lining edges will be even, with the zipper sandwiched between them.

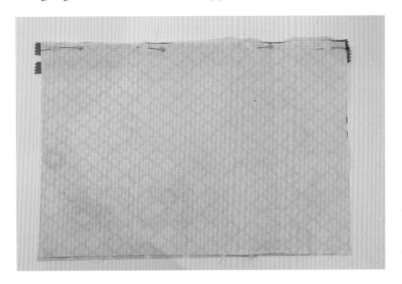

5. Stitch using your zipper foot. Repeat with the other side of the zipper, using the back and remaining lining piece.

6. Unzip the zipper. Match the front and back pieces with right sides together. Match the lining pieces with right sides together.

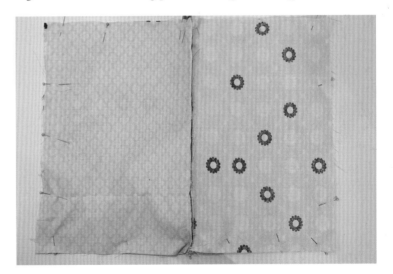

7. Stitch all around the outside, leaving a 3″ opening in the bottom of the pouch lining. Turn right side out and press. Machine stitch the opening closed in the pouch lining. Push the lining into the pouch.

Finishing Touches

LAYERING

Spread the backing wrong side up and tape the edges down with masking tape. (If you are working on carpet you can use T-pins to secure the backing to the carpet.) Center the batting on top, smoothing out any folds. Place the quilt top right side up on top of the batting and backing, making sure it is centered.

BASTING

Basting keeps the quilt "sandwich" layers from shifting while you are quilting.

If you plan to machine quilt, pin baste the quilt layers together with safety pins placed a minimum of 3″–4″ apart. Begin basting in the center and move toward the edges first in vertical, then horizontal, rows. Try not to pin directly on the intended quilting lines.

If you plan to hand quilt, baste the layers together with thread using a long needle and light-colored thread. Knot one end of the thread. Using stitches approximately the length of the needle, begin in the center and move out toward the edges in vertical and horizontal rows approximately 4″ apart. Add 2 diagonal rows of basting.

QUILTING

Quilting, whether by hand or machine, enhances the pieced or appliquéd design of the quilt. You may choose to quilt in-the-ditch, echo the pieced or appliqué motifs, use patterns from quilting design books and stencils, or do your own free-motion quilting. Remember to check your batting manufacturer's recommendations for how close the quilting lines must be.

BINDING

Trim excess batting and backing from the quilt even with the edges of the quilt top.

Double Fold Straight Grain Binding

If you want a ¼″ finished binding, cut the binding strips 2″ wide and piece them together with diagonal seams to make a continuous binding strip. Trim the seam allowance to ¼″. Press the seams open.

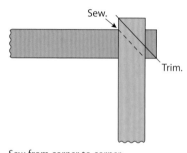

Sew from corner to corner.

Completed diagonal seam

Press the entire strip in half lengthwise with wrong sides together. With raw edges even, pin the binding to the front edge of the quilt a few inches away from the corner, and leave the first few inches of the binding unattached. Start sewing, using a ¼″ seam allowance.

Stop ¼″ away from the first corner (see Step 1), backstitch one stitch. Lift the presser foot and needle. Rotate the quilt one-quarter turn. Fold the binding at a right angle so it extends straight above the quilt and the fold forms a 45° angle in the corner (see Step 2).

Then bring the binding strip down even with the edge of the quilt (see Step 3). Begin sewing at the folded edge. Repeat in the same manner at all corners.

Step 1. Stitch to ¼″ from corner.

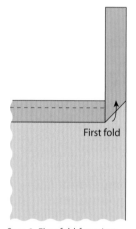

Step 2. First fold for miter

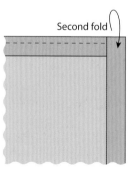

Step 3. Second fold alignment

Continue stitching until you are back near the beginning of the binding strip. See Finishing the Binding Ends for tips on finishing and hiding the raw edges of the ends of the binding.

Finishing the Binding Ends

Method 1: After stitching around the quilt, fold under the beginning tail of the binding strip ¼″ so that the raw edge will be inside the binding after it is turned to the backside of the quilt. Place the end tail of the binding strip over the beginning folded end. Continue to attach the binding and stitch slightly beyond the starting stitches. Trim the excess binding. Fold the binding over the raw edges to the quilt back and hand stitch, mitering the corners.

Method 2: (See our blog entry at ctpubblog.com, search for "invisible seam," then scroll down to "Quilting Tips: Completing a Binding With an Invisible Seam.")

Fold the ending tail of the binding back on itself where it meets the beginning binding tail. From the fold, measure and mark the cut width of your binding strip. Cut the ending binding tail to this measurement. For example, if your binding is cut 2⅛″ wide, measure from the fold on the ending tail of the binding 2⅛″ and cut the binding tail to this length.

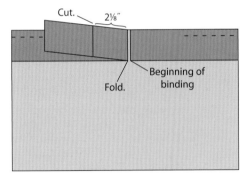

Cut binding tail.

Open both tails. Place one tail on top of the other tail at right angles, right sides together. Mark a diagonal line from corner to corner and stitch on the line. Check that you've done it correctly and that the binding fits the quilt, then trim the seam allowance to ¼″. Press open.

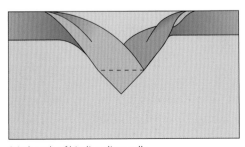

Stitch ends of binding diagonally.

Refold the binding and stitch this binding section in place on the quilt. Fold the binding over the raw edges to the quilt back and hand stitch.

Meet the Chefs...

John Q. Adams
quiltdad.com

Lissa Alexander
modalissa.blogspot.com

Natalia Bonner
piecenquilt.com
piecenquilt.blogspot.com

Vanessa Christenson
vanessachristenson.com

Vickie Eapen
spunsugarquilt.com

Jenny Garland
jennygarland.com

Rachel Griffith
www.psiquilt.com

Julie Herman
Jaybird Quilts
jaybirdquilts.com

Roslyn Mirrington
bloomandblossom.blogspot.com

For more great projects and inspiration check out our chef's fabulous sites!

Melissa Mortenson
polkadotchair.blogspot.com

Amanda Jean Nyberg
crazymomquilts.blogspot.com

Monica Solorio-Snow
thehappyzombie.com
flickr.com/photos/thehappyzombie
twitter.com/Happy_Zombie

Sweetwater
sweetwaterscrapbook.com
sweetwater.typepad.com
sweetwaterstreet.com

Kimberly Walus
bittybitsandpieces.blogspot.com

Angela Yosten
angelayosten.com

stashBOOKS

fabric arts for a handmade lifestyle

If you're craving beautiful authenticity in a time of mass-production...Stash Books is for you. Stash Books is a new line of how-to books celebrating fabric arts for a handmade lifestyle. Backed by C&T Publishing's solid reputation for quality, Stash Books will inspire you with contemporary designs, clear and simple instructions, and engaging photography.

www.stashbooks.com